SRA

Reading Mastery

Signature Edition

Language Arts Answer Key
Grade 3

Siegfried Engelmann
Jerry Silbert
Susan Hanner

Columbus, OH

SRAonline.com

 SRA

Send all inquiries to this address:
SRA/McGraw-Hill
8787 Orion Place
Columbus, OH 43240-4027

ISBN: 978-0-07-612611-8
MHID: 0-07-612611-0

5 6 7 8 9 10 11 12 GLO 17 16 15 14 13 12

The **McGraw·Hill** Companies

Workbook

A

1. The boy was from New York.	reports	(does not report)
2. A boy sat on the dock and fished.	(reports)	does not report
3. The boy wanted to be a boxer.	reports	(does not report)
4. The girl wore a red swimsuit.	reports	(does not report)
5. The girl sat in an inner tube.	(reports)	does not report
6. The girl liked to swim.	reports	(does not report)
7. The water was very warm.	reports	(does not report)
8. Several fish fell out of the bucket.	(reports)	does not report

B

1. jump __jumped__   3. bark __barked__   5. pick __picked__
2. pull __pulled__   4. push __pushed__   6. burn __burned__

C

1. find	*found*	6. buy	*bought*	11. dig	*dug*
2. give	*gave*	7. find	*found*	12. buy	*bought*
3. buy	*bought*	8. dig	*dug*	13. has	*had*
4. dig	*dug*	9. has	*had*	14. give	*gave*
5. has	*had*	10. give	*gave*	15. find	*found*

D

1. __An alligator__ ran into the room.
2. __Kevin__ stood behind his desk.
3. __The teacher__ made marks on a piece of paper.
4. __Ann__ watched the alligator from the front row.

E Circle the part of each sentence that names.

(An old cowboy) went to town.
(That cowboy) rode his horse to town.
(He) went to town to buy food.
(He) rode his horse to the food store.
(The cowboy) went inside.
(He) bought the food that he needed.

F

	Part F
1.	*Maria and her sister went to*
	the store.
2.	*My friend had a cold.*
3.	*The class went to the*
	lunchroom.
4.	*His bike had a flat tire.*

Student's name
Lesson 1

Part F
(Copied sentences should have correct
spelling, begin with capitals, start at
the margin and end with periods.)

A

Mrs. Lee

1. Mrs. Lee talked to her sister.   reports   (does not report)
2. The baby sat on a rug.   (reports)   does not report
3. The baby had just learned how to walk.   reports   (does not report)
4. The cat reached toward the birdcage.   (reports)   does not report
5. The cat was seven years old.   reports   (does not report)
6. The dog liked to play with the baby.   reports   (does not report)
7. The baby held on to the dog's tail.   (reports)   does not report
8. Mrs. Lee was making a birthday cake.   reports   (does not report)

B   Circle the part of each sentence that names.

(A little gray cat) looked for its owner. (It) looked and looked. (The poor cat) was hungry. (The cat) made a lot of noise. (It) went up one street and down another. (The cat) found its owner. (That little cat) felt very happy.

C   Fill in each blank with *He, She* or *It*.

1. The car broke down.   1. ___It___ broke down.
2. The dream went on for an hour.   2. ___It___ went on for an hour.
3. The young boy sat in a chair.   3. ___He___ sat in a chair.
4. The monkey was laughing.   4. ___It___ was laughing.
5. My older sister helped me.   5. ___She___ helped me.
6. The pen fell off the table.   6. ___It___ fell off the table.

D

1.

The firefighter

- The firefighter is chopping a hole in the door.
- The firefighter was chopping a hole in the door.
- The firefighter chopped a hole in the door.

The firefighter chopped a hole in the door.

2.

Sally

- Sally is diving into the pool.
- Sally dove into the pool.
- Sally was diving into the pool.

Sally dove into the pool.

3.

Latrell

- Latrell ate a sandwich.
- Latrell was eating a sandwich.
- Latrell is eating a sandwich.

Latrell ate a sandwich.

4.

The girl

- The girl was painting the wall.
- The girl is painting the wall.
- The girl painted the wall.

The girl painted the wall.

E

1. The boy ~~was eating~~ **ate** lunch.
2. The girl ~~is running~~ **ran** home.
3. The boy ~~was playing~~ **played** soccer.
4. He ~~is drinking~~ **drank** water.
5. She ~~was driving~~ **drove** a bus.

| drank | drove | ate | played | ran |

F

Part F

    Pedro had a very smart dog. The dog could do many tricks. It could walk on its back legs. It could jump through a hoop. All of the children liked to play with the. smart dog.

(Copied paragraph should have correct spelling, the first line indented, with the other lines beginning at the margin. Each sentence starts with a capital and ends with a period.)

2

A   Fill in each blank with *He, She* or *It*.

1. The shirt was covered with dirt.   1. ___It___ was covered with dirt.
2. The rubber ball fell off the table.   2. ___It___ fell off the table.
3. The man sat in a chair.   3. ___He___ sat in a chair.
4. The book was very funny.   4. ___It___ was very funny.
5. The young woman rode a bike.   5. ___She___ rode a bike.
6. The game ended at four o'clock.   6. ___It___ ended at four o'clock.

B   Circle the part of each sentence that names.

(An old red bike) sat in the yard for years. (That bike) became rusty. (It) had spiderwebs on the wheels. (A girl) decided to fix up the bike. (She) painted the bike bright red. (She) put new tires on the bike. (The bike) looked great. (The girl) liked the bike.

C

A bull chased Pam through a field. Pam jumped over a fence. ~~And then~~ T the bull jumped over the fence. ~~And~~ Pam kept on running. ~~And~~ T the bull was right behind her. Pam ran over to a tree. ~~And then~~ S she climbed up the tree as fast as she could. ~~And~~ T the bull waited under the tree until the sun went down. ~~And then~~ Pam climbed down after the bull left. ~~And~~ S she knew she shouldn't have taken a shortcut through that field.

D   Fix up each sentence so that it tells what the person or thing did.

1. He ~~was taking~~ *took* a bath.
2. They ~~were looking~~ *looked* at the sky.
3. The dog ~~was licking~~ *licked* my face.
4. She ~~is building~~ *built* a fire.
5. The teacher ~~was sitting~~ *sat* on a chair.
6. She ~~is folding~~ *folded* the paper.

built	folded	licked	looked	sat	took

E

1. Norma
2. Yancy

- Norma was sawing a board.
- Norma is sawing a board.
- (Norma sawed a board.)

- Yancy was trying to ride a horse.
- (Yancy tried to ride a horse.)
- Yancy is trying to ride a horse.

(✓ margin ✓ capitals ✓ periods ✓ vocabulary box spelling)
1. (Sentence reports on main thing James did.)
2. (Sentence reports on main thing a girl did.)

F   Write sentences that report on the main thing each person did.

1. James

2. A girl

3. Robert

3. (Sentence reports on main thing Robert did.)

board	teeth	brushed	kicked	erased	football

G

	Part G
	Jason had a bad day. He
	missed breakfast because he
	woke up late. He had to walk to
	school in the rain.
	☐1 ☐2 ☐3

Check 1: Does each sentence begin with a capital and end with a period?
Check 2: Did you spell all the words correctly?
Check 3: Did you indent the first line and start all the other lines at the margin?
Part G
(Copied paragraph: ✓ capitals and periods ✓ all words spelled correctly ✓ indented first line only)
✓1 ✓2 ✓3

A   Circle the part of each sentence that names.

(A hungry little cat) walked into a restaurant. (It) wanted something to eat. (A nice woman) owned the restaurant. (She) gave the cat a bowl of milk. (The little animal) drank every drop of milk. (The woman) liked the cat. (She) made a little bed for it. (The cat) had a new home.

B

Tom threw a snowball at his friend. ~~And~~ I it hit his friend's leg. ~~And then~~ H his friend chased him. ~~And~~ T they both ran as fast as they could. His friend caught Tom in the middle of the park. ~~And then~~ Tom told his friend that he was sorry for hitting him in the leg with the snowball. The boys shook hands. ~~And~~ T they were still friends.

C Fill in the blank next to each sentence with *He, She, It* or *They.*

1. The man and the woman ate lunch.
2. Latrell and Kedrick walked on the sand.
3. The truck had a flat tire.
4. The apples cost 84 cents.
5. The women wore red shirts.
6. The old book was worth a lot of money.
7. Alberto and his dog went jogging.
8. The old man wore a long blue coat.

1. __They__ ate lunch.
2. __They__ walked on the sand.
3. __It__ had a flat tire.
4. __They__ cost 84 cents.
5. __They__ wore red shirts.
6. __It__ was worth a lot of money.
7. __They__ went jogging.
8. __He__ wore a long blue coat.

D Fix up each sentence so that it tells what the persons did.

1. She ~~is riding~~ *rode* a horse.
2. The girls ~~were talking~~ *talked* loudly.
3. The men ~~are painting~~ *painted* the room.
4. He ~~was holding~~ *held* the baby.
5. She ~~is standing~~ *stood* on a chair.
6. They ~~were washing~~ *washed* the windows.

held	painted	rode	stood	talked	washed

E Fix up the passage so that all the sentences tell what the person did.

Marcus woke up late. He ~~was running~~ *ran* down the stairs. He grabbed his school book. He ~~is jumping~~ *jumped* onto his bike. He rode the bike as fast as he could. He ~~was parking~~ *parked* the bike. He ran into the classroom. He ~~was sitting~~ *sat* in his chair.

A Put in the capitals and periods. Circle the part of each sentence that names.

(A young boy) threw a ball. (the ball) went over his friend's head. (It) rolled into the street. (a big truck) ran over the ball. (the truck driver) gave the boys a new ball. (they) thanked the truck driver.

B

1. The workers fixed the house. ~~and~~ Two carpenters nailed boards over the broken windows. ~~and a~~ A plumber repaired the broken sink.
2. The girls rode their bikes to school. ~~and~~ Their friends took the bus to school. ~~and e~~ Everyone got to school on time.
3. The telephone rang six times. ~~and n~~ Nobody heard it. ~~and e~~ Everybody was outside in the yard.

C Fix up each sentence so that it tells what the persons did.

1. They ~~were wearing~~ *wore* helmets.
2. She ~~was throwing~~ *threw* the ball.
3. They ~~were cleaning~~ *cleaned* the room.
4. The boys ~~were sitting~~ *sat* on the floor.
5. He ~~was wearing~~ *wore* a new shirt.
6. The clown ~~was rubbing~~ *rubbed* his nose.

sat	threw	rubbed	wore	cleaned

D Fix up the passage so that all the sentences tell what the person did, not what the person was doing.

Jerry heard a noise. He ~~was seeing~~ *saw* a little kitten on the sidewalk. He picked up the kitten. He ~~was taking~~ *took* it home with him. He ~~was giving~~ *gave* it some water. He made a little bed for it. He loved his new pet.

E Fill in the blank next to each sentence with *He, She, It* or *They.*

1. A cat and a dog made a mess.
2. The girls went to school.
3. My mother was very pretty.
4. Rodney and his brother were not home.
5. Four ducks swam on the lake.
6. The tables were old.
7. My brother came home late.
8. That car was bright red.

1. __They__ made a mess.
2. __They__ went to school.
3. __She__ was very pretty.
4. __They__ were not home.
5. __They__ swam on the lake.
6. __They__ were old.
7. __He__ came home late.
8. __It__ was bright red.

F

	A bluebird sat on a tree branch. A
DID	*striped cat ~~was running~~* (ran) *up the trunk of*
	the tree to get the bird. The cat ran
CP	*toward the bird. The bird flew away.*
M	*The branch broke. ~~The cat held out its paws~~*
	The cat fell to the ground.

Check 1: Does each sentence tell the main thing? (M)
Check 2: Does each sentence begin with a capital and end with a period? (CP)
Check 3: Does each sentence tell what somebody or something did? (DID)

A   Put in the capitals and periods.

~~a~~(A) *boy took his mom to the movies.* ~~he~~(H) *had*
a good time.~~the~~(T) *movie was very funny,*
~~his~~(H) *mom bought a big box of popcorn.~~they~~*(T)
rode home on their bikes.

B   Fix up the passage so that no sentence begins with *and* or *and then*.

Richard had a good day. Richard's teacher gave Richard his report card just before the school day ended. ~~And~~ Richard jumped with joy when he saw the good marks on his report card. ~~And then~~ (H)he ran home to show his mother the report card. ~~And then~~ (H)he gave her the report card. ~~And then~~ (H)his mother read the report card for several minutes. ~~And~~ (S)she was so happy that she made Richard and the rest of the children a big pizza for dinner.

C   Fix up the run-on sentences.

1. The boy ran down the street. ~~and~~ (H)He held his books in his arms.
2. The girl ran into the room. ~~and~~ (S)she looked all over for her books. ~~and~~ (S)she didn't know where they could be.
3. The airplane flew above the clouds. ~~and~~ (I)it was about 60 miles from the airport. ~~and~~ (T)the pilot looked at the charts.
4. The boy walked slowly to the store. ~~and~~ (H)He stopped three times to talk to his friends. ~~and~~ (T)the store was closed when the boy got there.
5. Rosa wrote a funny story about alligators. ~~and~~ (S)she read it to the class. ~~and~~ (T)the children liked her story very much.
6. The dog did a trick. ~~and~~ (I)it walked in circles on its back legs. ~~and~~ (T)the boy gave the dog a snack for doing such a good trick.

D   Fix up each sentence so that it tells what the person or thing did.

1. The boy ~~was chasing~~ (chased) a dog.
2. The girl ~~was washing~~ (washed) the car.
3. He ~~was writing~~ (wrote) a letter.
4. She ~~was eating~~ (ate) apples.
5. The airplane ~~was taking~~ (took) off.

took	chased	wrote	ate	washed

E   Circle the subject. Underline the part that tells more.

1. (Three older boys) went to the store.
2. (A horse and a dog) went to a stream.
3. (A man) sat on a log.
4. (They) sat on a bench.
5. (My friend and his mother) were hungry.
6. (My hands and my face) got dirty.

A Put in the capitals and periods.

> *A* girl threw a ball to her brother. *S*he
> threw the ball too hard. *I*t rolled into the
> street. *T*he boy started to run into the
> street. *A* truck moved toward the boy. *A*
> woman saw the truck. *S*he grabbed the boy.
> *T*he truck ran over the ball. *T*he woman told
> the boy to be more careful.

B Fill in the blanks with **He, She** or **It**.

1. Robert spent all morning cleaning his room. <u>He</u> put his dirty clothes into the laundry basket. <u>He</u> washed the floor and the windows.

2. My sister went to the park. <u>She</u> played basketball with her friends for two hours. <u>She</u> scored 20 points.

3. The boat went around the small lake. <u>It</u> had three sails. <u>It</u> moved very quickly across the water.

E Circle the subject of each sentence. Underline the part that tells more.

1. (A jet airplane) made a lot of noise.
2. (A man and his dog) went walking.
3. (He) ate lunch in the office.
4. (My brother and his friend) played in the park.
5. (A little cat) drank milk.

F

CP	A cowboy fell off a bull. *A* bull charged
DID	at the cowboy. A clown ~~was putting~~ *put* a
M	barrel in front of the bull. ^ The clown
	helped the cowboy walk away from the bull.
	Idea: The bull hit the barrel into the air.

Check 1: Does each sentence tell the main thing? (M)
Check 2: Does each sentence begin with a capital and end with a period? (CP)
Check 3: Does each sentence tell what somebody or something did? (DID)

C

1. Alberto ate lunch in the kitchen. ~~and~~ *H*e ate two cheese sandwiches covered with mustard. ~~and~~ *H*e got mustard all over his face and shirt.

2. The girl looked out the window at the snow. ~~and~~ *S*he did not like cold weather. ~~and~~ *S*he wished that she lived in a warmer place.

3. The dog ran down the street. ~~and~~ *I*t barked at a truck. ~~and~~ *T*he truck driver waved at the dog.

4. My friend did not feel well. ~~and~~ *S*he had a fever. ~~and~~ *H*er mother kept her home from school.

5. The dish fell off the table. ~~and~~ *I*t broke into many pieces. ~~and~~ *T*he boy swept up the pieces.

6. Rodney listened to the voice on the telephone. ~~and~~ *H*e didn't know who was speaking. ~~and~~ *T*he voice sounded strange.

D Fix up each sentence so that it tells what the person did.

1. The men ~~were telling~~ *told* jokes.
2. She ~~was picking~~ *picked* up the pencils.
3. They ~~were washing~~ *washed* the car.
4. He ~~was sitting~~ *sat* on a log.
5. She ~~was painting~~ *painted* the wall.

painted	told	sat	washed	picked

A Fix up the run-on sentences in this passage.

A girl got a big dog for her birthday. ~~and~~ *T*he dog was so big that it could not fit through the doors of the girl's house. It had to live outside in a house with big doors. The dog followed the girl to the school bus stop one morning. ~~and~~ *T*he girl didn't see the dog behind her. ~~and~~ *T*he dog tried to sneak onto the bus. The door of the bus was too small. The dog got stuck. ~~and~~ *A*ll the children had to push together to get the dog off the bus.

B Fix up the passage so that each sentence begins with a capital and ends with a period.

> *A* man took a big egg out of a nest. The
> man brought the egg to his house. *H*e
> thought that the egg might be worth a lot
> of money. The doorbell rang. *T*he man walked
> to the door. He opened the door. *A* big bird
> flew into the room. It picked up the egg.
> *T*he man fainted. The big bird flew away with
> the egg.

Lesson 8

C   Edit the passage for these checks:

Check 1: Do any sentences begin with *and* or *and then?*
Check 2: Do all the words that are part of a person's name begin with a capital?

Tonya Jackson was playing baseball. And her team was losing two to one. Tonya was at bat. The pitcher threw the ball to Tonya. Tonya swung. She missed the ball. And Tonya was mad. The pitcher threw the ball toward Tonya again. And then Tonya swung. She hit the ball. And It went far over everybody's head. Tonya ran around the bases. Her team won the game. And then All the girls clapped for Tonya.

D   Cross out some of the names and write *He, She* or *It*.

(A) Mario found many things when he went walking. (B) Mario He once found a striped cat. (C) That cat was very thin. (D) That cat It was sitting on the sidewalk. (E) Mario took the cat home with him. (F) Mario He tried to hide the cat from his mother. (G) His mother heard the cat. (H) His mother She liked the cat and told Mario that he could keep it.

E   Circle the subject of each sentence. Underline the predicate.

1. (Five cats) were on the roof.
2. (They) read two funny books.
3. (A red bird) landed on a roof.
4. (A dog and a cat) played in their yard.
5. (It) stopped.

Lesson 9

A   Fix up the run-on sentences in this passage.

Tom made some chocolate cookies. and He put them in a shoe box. and He put the shoe box in a corner of the kitchen. He went outside to play. Susan started cleaning the kitchen. and She did not know what was in the shoe box. and She threw the shoe box away. Tom got hungry. He went into the kitchen. He looked for the shoe box. It was gone. He asked Susan if she had seen the shoe box. and She told him she had thrown it away. Tom told Susan what was in the shoe box. Susan helped Tom make another batch of cookies.

B   Cross out some of the names and write *He, She* or *It*.

(A) Trina loved to look for things on the sidewalk. (B) Trina She found three bugs, two rocks and a baseball yesterday. (C) Her father did not like some of the things she found. (D) Her father He did not like the bugs that Trina brought home. (E) Trina's brother liked one of the things Trina found. (F) Trina's brother He liked the baseball.

C   Fix up the passage so that each sentence begins with a capital and ends with a period.

A man saw a butterfly. It had purple and white spots. The man wanted to catch the butterfly. He got a net. He started to chase the butterfly. It flew over a pond. The man fell into the pond. The pretty butterfly flew away.

D   If the words are somebody's name, begin the words with capital letters.

Lamar Jenkins   Mrs. Williams   the doctor   his brother
Tyrell Washington   Jerry Martinez   this boy   Mr. Garcia
          the girl   the nurse   Mrs. Cash

E   Fix up the passage so that all the sentences tell what a person did, not what a person was doing.

Shameka bought a little tree. She was digging dug a hole in her yard. She put the tree into the hole. She was filling filled the hole with dirt. She was watering watered the tree. She built a little fence around the tree.

F   Circle the subject of each sentence. Underline the predicate.

1. (Sara and Harry) painted the kitchen blue.
2. (Sara) had a paintbrush.
3. (Harry) used a roller.
4. (They) stopped to eat lunch.
5. (She) laughed.
6. (The windows) were blue.

G

DID	Jill threw a ball to Robert. Robert ~~jump~~ jumped
	up to catch the ball. The ball went over
CP	Robert's head. it rolled down the hill
	toward a skunk. Rover chased the ball.
M	^Robert and Jill held their noses.
	Idea: The skunk made a big stink.

Check 1: Does each sentence tell the main thing? (M)
Check 2: Does each sentence begin with a capital and end with a period? (CP)
Check 3: Does each sentence tell what somebody or something did? (DID)

A   Fix up the run-on sentences.

1. Mr. Clark went for a ride in the country. ~~and then~~ His car ran out of gas. ~~and then~~ He had to walk three miles to a gas station.

2. Kathy liked to read books. ~~and~~ Her favorite book was about horses. ~~and~~ Her brother gave her that book.

3. Pam's mother asked Pam to mow the lawn. ~~and then~~ Pam started to cut the grass. ~~and~~ It was too wet.

B   Cross out some of the names, and write *he, she* or *it.*

James had a birthday yesterday. ~~James~~ He was 11 years old. His mother brought a big birthday cake to school. ~~His mother~~ She gave a piece of cake to each person in James' class. The cake tasted great. ~~The cake~~ It had chocolate icing.

TEST 1   Test Score [ ]

A   Put in the capitals and periods.

My older sister took her dog to the park. Her dog chased a skunk. The skunk got mad. It made a terrible stink. My sister had to wash her dog for hours to get rid of the smell.

B   Fix up the sentences so they tell what people did.

1. He ~~was giving~~ gave me a pen.
2. He ~~was buying~~ bought a shirt.
3. They ~~were picking~~ picked flowers.
4. He ~~is filling~~ filled the glass.
5. My friend ~~is having~~ had a party.
6. A boy ~~is spelling~~ spelled words.

gave	bought

C   Fill in the blanks with **He, She, It** or **They.**

1. Two girls ate lunch.
2. A cow and a horse slept in the barn.
3. His sister went home.
4. The blue pen fell off the desk.
5. James is sick today.
6. My friends went to a party.

1. ___They___ ate lunch.
2. ___They___ slept in the barn.
3. ___She___ went home.
4. ___It___ fell off the desk.
5. ___He___ is sick today.
6. ___They___ went to a party.

D   Circle the subject of each sentence. Underline the predicate.

1. (A young man) walked home.
2. (It) made a big noise.
3. (My little sister) is sick.
4. (Her brother and sister) went to school.
5. (That pencil) belongs to her.

Lesson 11

A Fill in the blanks with the correct words.

Three women worked on a house.
___They___ wore work clothes.
___Milly___ cut a board. ___She___
used a saw. ___Kay___ carried three
pieces of wood. ___She___ carried the
boards on her shoulder. ___Jean___
hammered nails into the wood.

B Fix up the run-on sentences.

1. Miss Wilson saw a used bike at a store. ~~and~~ T̶he bike was red and blue. ~~and then~~ Miss Wilson bought it for her sister. (3)

2. Richard and his sister went to a movie. ~~and~~ I̶t was very funny. ~~and~~ Richard and his sister ate popcorn. ~~and then~~ T̶heir mother picked them up after the movie. (4)

3. Tina built a doghouse for her dog. ~~and then~~ S̶he looked in the doghouse. ~~and~~ F̶our cats were in the doghouse with her dog. (3)

C Circle the subject of each sentence. Underline the predicate. Then make a **V** above the verb.

1. (Six bottles) were on the table.
2. (An old lion) chased the rabbit.
3. (Jane and Sue) sat under a tree.
4. (His brother) had a candy bar.

D

A woman lived near our school. Her name was m̲rs. j̲ones. s̲he was an airplane pilot. She told us many stories about flying planes.

☐ **Check 1.** Does each sentence begin with a capital and end with a period?
☐ **Check 2.** Does each part of a person's name begin with a capital letter?

Lesson 12

A

1. (A black pencil) fell off the table.
2. (My sister) was sick.
3. (A dog and a cat) played in the park.
4. (They) smiled.
5. (Mary) sang softly.
6. (An old horse) drank from a bucket.

B Fix up the run-on sentences in this paragraph.

Don found a lost dog. ~~and~~ T̶he dog had a collar around its neck. The collar had a phone number on it. ~~and then~~ Don called the phone number. ~~and~~ T̶he dog's owner answered the telephone. The owner was happy that Don found the dog. He went to Don's house. ~~and then~~ Don gave the dog to the owner.

C For each verb that tells what somebody does, write the verb that tells what somebody did.

1. begins   ___began___
2. brings   ___brought___
3. flies   ___flew___
4. swims   ___swam___
5. takes   ___took___
6. comes   ___came___

D Fill in the blanks with the correct words.

___Ben___ sat in the
wheelchair. ___He___ wore pajamas.
The ___wheelchair___ had big wheels and
little wheels. ___It___ had a seat,
a back and two handles. ___Dora___
held a purse. ___She___ wore a skirt
and a sweater. ___Ruth___ was behind
the wheelchair. ___She___ pushed the wheelchair.

E

	A little bird fell out of its nest.
DID	James ~~pick~~ picked up the little bird. His
M	sister climbed up the tree. ^
CP	S̶he put the bird back in its nest.
	Idea: James handed the bird to his sister.

Check 1: Does each sentence tell the main thing? (M)
Check 2: Does each sentence begin with a capital and end with a period? (CP)
Check 3: Does each sentence tell what somebody or something did? (DID)

9

A

1. (She) jumped into the pool. [V]
2. (A young woman) read a book about dinosaurs. [V]
3. (My mother) had a new car. [V]
4. (They) laughed. [V]
5. (My brother and my sister) ate cookies and ice cream. [V]

B

Linda went on an airplane. ~~and~~ She had never been on an airplane before. [S] She sat in a seat next to the window. ~~and~~ The plane took off. [T] She fell asleep for an hour. ~~and~~ She woke up. ~~and~~ The plane landed. [S] [T] Her grandmother was waiting for her.

C Fill in the blanks with the correct words.

James and Alice worked in the garden. They wore work clothes. Alice dug a hole. She pushed the shovel down with her foot. James sawed a branch. He held the branch with one hand.

James
Alice

A Fix up the run-on sentences in the paragraph.

Jessica and Mark bought a pumpkin for Halloween. ~~and~~ The pumpkin [T] was so big that they could not carry it home. They started to roll it home. They pushed the pumpkin up a steep hill. ~~and then~~ Mark slipped. The pumpkin rolled down the hill. It smashed into a tree. ~~and~~ Jessica and Mark had lots of pumpkin pie the next day.

B

1. walked	2. smiled	3. picked	4. cried
was walking	was smiling	was picking	was crying

C Write the missing word in each item.

1. the hat that belongs to the boy — the __boy's__ hat
2. the bone that belongs to the dog — the __dog's__ bone
3. the car that belongs to her father — her __father's__ car
4. the arm that belongs to the girl — the __girl's__ arm
5. the book that belongs to my friend — my __friend's__ book
6. the toy that belongs to the cat — the __cat's__ toy

D

corner	licking	floor	boy's hand	sitting

1.   2.

Circle the name of each thing that is different in picture 1 and picture 2.

(the glass)   bowl of fruit   (boy)   pajamas

(cat)   (milk in the glass)   wall

A Fix up the run-on sentences in the paragraph.

Ronald put his finger in a bottle. ~~and~~ His finger got stuck in the bottle. ~~and~~ [H] ~~then~~ He asked his sister to help him. His sister got some butter. ~~and then~~ She [H] [S] rubbed the butter around the top of the bottle. She pulled on the bottle. ~~and~~ ~~then~~ His finger came out. [H]

B Circle the subject. Underline the predicate. Make a **V** above every verb.

1. (The boy) walked to the store. [V]
   (The boy) was walking to the store. [V]
2. (Two girls) ate candy. [V]
   (Two girls) were eating candy. [V]
3. (A fish) swam in the bathtub. [V]
   (A fish) was swimming in the bathtub. [V] [V]

C Write the missing word in each item.

1. the dress that belongs to the girl — the __girl's__ dress
2. the tent that belongs to her friend — her __friend's__ tent
3. the toy that belongs to my cat — my __cat's__ toy
4. the watch that belongs to that boy — that __boy's__ watch
5. the hammer that belongs to his mother — his __mother's__ hammer
6. the leg that belongs to my father — my __father's__ leg

| lying | sitting | horse | ground | running away |

1. 2.

Circle the name of each thing that is different in picture 1 and picture 2.

(the horse)   (boy)   boy's hat   (cowboy)

(the cowboy's hat)   mountain

B Circle the subject. Underline the predicate. Make a **V** above every verb.

1. (The young woman) walked to the school.
   (The young woman) was walking to the school.
2. (The children) smiled at the clown.
   (The children) were smiling at the clown.
3. (Mark and Jenny) raked the leaves.
   (Mark and Jenny) were raking the leaves.
4. (They) swam in the lake.
   (They) were swimming in the lake.

C Fix up the run-on sentences.

1. The boy went to the store and bought groceries.
2. The boy went to the store. and then His sister bought groceries.
3. My brother mowed the lawn and swept the sidewalk.
4. My brother mowed the lawn. and then He swept the sidewalk later.
5. The workers started early. and Their boss went home late.
6. The workers started early and went home late.
7. She ran up the stairs and went inside the house.
8. She ran up the stairs. and She went inside.

D Rewrite each item with an apostrophe **s**.

1. The shirt belonged to **that boy**. The shirt was red.
   _____That boy's shirt_____ was red.
2. The tail belonged to **a lion**. The tail was long.
   _____A lion's tail_____ was long.
3. The desk belonged to **my teacher**. The desk was old.
   _____My teacher's desk_____ was old.
4. The hand belonged to **his mother**. The hand was sore.
   _____His mother's hand_____ was sore.
5. The car belonged to **my sister**. The car was dented.
   _____My sister's car_____ was dented.

E

CP	A truck went over a rock.
	A barrel fell out of the truck. The
DID	barrel <s>roll down</s> rolled a hill. It crashed
WH	into a tree. ^ The boy caught the
RO	apple. <s>and</s> He gave it to a teacher.
	Idea: An apple fell from the tree.

Check 1: Did you give a clear picture of what happened? (WH)
Check 2: Did you fix up any run-on sentences? (RO)
Check 3: Does each sentence begin with a capital and end with a period? (CP)
Check 4: Does each sentence tell what somebody or something did? (DID)

A Fix up the run-on sentences.

1. Melissa fed her dog. and She went inside to change her shoes.
2. Ann loved horses. and Her big brother wanted a horse for his birthday.
3. The children went to the farm and played with the animals.
4. My brother swept the floor and washed the dishes.
5. A man and a woman watched TV. and He had a sore arm.
6. Ron went to the park and fed the birds.

B Rewrite each item with an apostrophe **s**.

1. The pencil belonged to **a girl**. The pencil was yellow.
   _____A girl's pencil_____ was yellow.
2. The nest belonged to **that bird**. The nest had eggs in it.
   _____That bird's nest_____ had eggs in it.
3. The glasses belonged to **my friend**. The glasses were broken.
   _____My friend's glasses_____ were broken.
4. The bottle belonged to **her baby**. The bottle had milk in it.
   _____Her baby's bottle_____ had milk in it.

Lesson 18

A Fix up the run-on sentences in this paragraph.

 Tom stopped in front of the pet shop and looked in the window. He saw
 T
a puppy inside. ~~and~~ ~~the~~ the pet store was open. ~~and~~ Tom didn't have any money to
buy the puppy. He wanted the puppy. ~~and He~~ He went home to talk to his parents.
 H
They told him he could have the puppy. Tom did jobs. ~~and then He~~ He earned the
 H
money he needed to buy the puppy.

B Rewrite each item with an apostrophe **s.**

1. The car belonged to **Tom.** The car was new.
   _____Tom's car_____ was new.

2. The wheel belonged to **his bike.** The wheel was bent.
   _____His bike's wheel_____ was bent.

3. The motor belonged to **that truck.** The motor made a lot of noise.
   _____That truck's motor_____ made a lot of noise.

4. The finger belonged to **Sally.** The finger was swollen.
   _____Sally's finger_____ was swollen.

5. The mouth belonged to **the dog.** The mouth was sore.
   _____The dog's mouth_____ was sore.

C Write sentences that tell what must have happened in the middle picture. Tell about **the horse, Bill** and **Lisa.**

| corral | grabbed | fence | rail |

D

RO	A gorilla escaped from its cage. ~~and~~ ~~the~~ The
	zookeeper made a trail of bananas that led
DID	back to the cage. The gorilla ~~follow the~~ followed
	zookeeper. It picked up the bananas and
WH	started to eat them. ^The zookeeper
	closed the gate behind the gorilla.
	Idea: The gorilla walked into the cage.

Check 1: Did you give a clear picture of what happened? (WH)
Check 2: Did you fix up any run-on sentences? (RO)
Check 3: Does each sentence begin with a capital and end with a period? (CP)
Check 4: Does each sentence tell what somebody or something did? (DID)

Lesson 20

A

RO	Alex threw a frisbee to his dog. ~~and~~ ~~the~~ The
	frisbee went over the dog's head. A bear cub
WH	grabbed the frisbee. ^The mother bear
DID	heard the barking and ~~walk~~ walked into the
	field. Alex picked up his dog and ran to
CP	a big tree.
	Idea: The dog barked at the bear cub.

Check 1: Did you give a clear picture of what happened? (WH)
Check 2: Did you fix up any run-on sentences? (RO)
Check 3: Does each sentence begin with a capital and end with a period? (CP)
Check 4: Does each sentence tell what somebody or something did? (DID)

TEST 2 Test Score [ ] **Lesson 20**

A Read the paragraph. Fix up any run-ons.

 A turtle and a rabbit had a race. ~~and~~ ~~the~~ The rabbit ran very fast. The turtle
 T
could not run fast. The rabbit saw a garden full of carrots. ~~and then~~ The rabbit
 T
stopped and ate lots of carrots. The turtle kept on running. ~~and~~ The turtle won
 T
the race. ~~and then~~ The rabbit got mad because he lost the race.
 T

B Write the verb for each sentence.

1. The red pencil fell on the floor. _____fell_____
2. My little brother was sleeping under the bed. _____was sleeping_____
3. The bus had eight wheels. _____had_____
4. My brother and my sister were running up the stairs. _____were running_____
5. They stopped. _____stopped_____
6. We found a little dog. _____found_____

C Rewrite each item with an apostrophe **s**.

1. The shirt belonged to **Tom.** The shirt was dirty.

   _____Tom's shirt_____ was dirty.

2. The dog belonged to **his sister.** The dog was barking.

   _____His sister's dog_____ was barking.

3. The toy belonged to **the baby.** The toy was on the bed.

   _____The baby's toy_____ was on the bed.

4. The motor belonged to **that car.** The motor made a loud noise.

   _____That car's motor_____ made a loud noise.

D Fill in the blanks with the correct words.

The men went fishing. ___They___

were in a boat in the middle of the lake.

___Ken___ sat in the middle of the

boat. ___Pete___ held a fishing pole

in one hand and a net in the other hand.

___He___ sat in the back of the boat.

___Al___ stood in the front of the boat.

___He___ smiled as his fishing pole bent.

A

1. Milly played baseball with Linda. ~~She~~ **Milly** threw the ball.

2. Milly played baseball with Jeff. ~~Milly~~ She threw the ball.

3. Gary and John went to the store. ~~He~~ **John** had been working all day.

4. Jessica talked to Liz. **Jessica** ~~She~~ was walking home.

5. Kathy handed a glass to Bill. ~~Kathy~~ She told him where to put it.

B Circle all the words in column 4 that are verbs.

1	2	3	4
ran	girls	cried	(went)
talked	stove	bought	bird
turned	brother	house	(walked)
yelled	pretty	whispered	(flew)
sat	quietly	teacher	pretty
smiled	man	yellow	(slept)
fell	lazy	swam	(sold)

A

1. Tom waved to Martha. ~~Martha~~ She was riding a horse.

2. Larry wanted to meet James. **Larry** ~~He~~ had a new bike.

3. Barbara gave her sister a rabbit. **Her sister** ~~She~~ loved rabbits.

4. Mr. Ross and Mr. Long were teachers. **Mr. Ross** ~~He~~ taught math.

5. Bill went fishing with Linda. ~~Linda~~ She caught four fish.

6. Ann and her mother went to a party. **Ann** ~~She~~ carried a cake.

B

1. six <u>chairs</u>
2. my father's <u>chairs</u>
3. my father's <u>chair</u>
4. some <u>apples</u>
5. that tree's <u>leaves</u>
6. a car's <u>headlights</u>
7. a boy's <u>kites</u>
8. two big <u>oranges</u>
9. those red <u>cars</u>
10. that boy's <u>books</u>
11. the teacher's <u>pencil</u>
12. the tallest <u>girls</u>

C Circle each word that is a verb.

(bought)   (smiled)   green   tall   (kicked)   (went)   boy

*See page 39 for Editing and Correcting a Paragraph answers.

A

1. Wendy and Debbie went to the beach. **Wendy** ~~She~~ flew her kite.

2. Robert and Dave walked home. **Dave** ~~He~~ carried a radio.

3. Tom and Pam walked to school. ~~Pam~~ She liked to walk fast.

4. Ed and Sam talked in the hall. **Ed** ~~He~~ stood near the door.

5. Linda helped Alice build a table. ~~Linda~~ She wanted to paint it red.

6. Ed asked Bob about school. **Ed** ~~He~~ had been absent for a week.

B

1. a girl's <u>hairbrush</u>
2. that cat's <u>tail</u>
3. the birds in the <u>tree</u>
4. the bugs on the <u>table</u>
5. those cats near <u>John</u>
6. an old man's <u>face</u>
7. the woman's <u>umbrella</u>
8. many <u>cups</u>
9. a girl's <u>suitcase</u>

A

1. Bill and Frank ate lunch. ~~Bill~~ **Bill** had a peanut butter sandwich.

2. Miss Winston and Miss Kelly were teachers. ~~She~~ **Miss Kelly** taught reading.

3. Kevin told Ann about a movie. ~~Kevin~~ **He** thought it was very funny.

4. My father gave Betty a book. ~~Betty~~ **She** liked to read books about space.

5. Tina sat next to Jane. ~~She~~ **Tina** was the smartest girl in class.

6. Wendy worked with Bill. ~~Wendy~~ **She** fixed a flat tire.

B | Change each sentence so the subject is a pronoun. Cross out the subject. Write the pronoun above it.

1. **He** ~~The old man~~ could not start the car.
2. **It** ~~A storm~~ lasted all night.
3. **They** ~~A dog and a cow~~ were eating.
4. **She** ~~The young woman~~ cleaned a table.
5. **They** ~~The trucks~~ went up the hill.
6. **She** ~~A mother~~ held a baby.

*See page 40 for Editing and Correcting a Paragraph answers.

A | Circle the subject in each sentence. Write **P** in front of every sentence that has a pronoun for a subject.

____ 1. (Donald) planted corn.
P 2. (It) had a broken handle.
P 3. (He) kicked a football.
____ 4. (Betty) baked three pies.

____ 5. (The truck) had 16 wheels.
P 6. (They) woke up late.
P 7. (She) planted corn.
____ 8. (Bugs) ran all over the table.

B

____**Ann**____ and ____**Kim**____ were swimming. ____**Ann**____ wore a bathing cap. ____**She**____ also wore a watch. ____**Jane**____ sat near the water. ____**She**____ wore sunglasses. ____**Sally**____ stood next to the blanket. ____**She**____ wore shorts. ____**She**____ read a book.

C

1. ~~The~~ **T**he boys ~~good~~ **went** to Bill's house. (3)
2. Alice fell asleep. **S**he was very tired. (2)
3. ~~That~~ **T**hat boy's shirt has six red buttons and four yellow buttons. (3)
4. My best friends are **J**erry **G**omez and **A**lex **J**ordan. (4)
5. Melissa and **R**ichard put their dog on **R**ichard's bed. (3)
6. We looked outside. ~~and~~ **T**he rain had just stopped. (2)

A | Circle the subject in each sentence. Write **P** in front of every sentence that has a pronoun for a subject.

____ 1. (The tree) was beautiful. **It**
P 2. (He) ate pizza for dinner.
____ 3. (Those dogs) chased our cat. **They**
____ 4. (Tina) read a book. **She**

P 5. (It) fell off the table.
P 6. (They) bought new shirts.
____ 7. (My sister) painted the room. **She**
____ 8. (Robert) finished his homework. **He**

B

____**Jerry/Al**____ and ____**Al/Jerry**____ picked apples from a tree. ____**Jerry**____ wore a hat. ____**He**____ had a beard. ____**Al**____ stood on a box. ____**He**____ held a bucket. ____**Sam/Bill**____ and ____**Bill/Sam**____ sat on a blanket. ____**Sam**____ read a book. ____**Bill**____ wore a shirt with the number 9 on the back. ____**He**____ drew a picture.

14

C

1. My dad's cat had four kittens. (2)
2. She ~~teached~~ taught R̲obert and J̲erry how to ride a bike. (3)
   taught R   J
3. S̲he washed the windows of her dad's car. (3)
4. We ~~seen~~ saw M̲rs. J̲ordan in the store. S̲he waved to us. (5)
   saw M J   S

*See page 42 for Editing and Correcting a
Paragraph answers.

A Circle the subject in each sentence. Write **P** in front of each sentence
that has a pronoun for a subject.

_____ 1. (Linda's shirt) was dirty. *It*

_P_ 2. (They) painted the door.

_P_ 3. (He) is ten years old.

_____ 4. (A new girl) walked into our class. *She*

_P_ 5. (It) had big tires.

_____ 6. (A boy and his friend) went to the store. *They*

_____ 7. (My little brother) is seven years old. *He*

_P_ 8. (She) walked to school.

B

Betty/Jane and Jane/Betty were playing basketball.
___Betty___ bounced a ball. ___She___ wore shorts and long socks.
___She___ wore a headband to keep her hair from getting in her eyes.
___Jane___ jumped into the air as she shot the ball toward the basket.
___Jane's mom___ leaned against a pole as she watched the girls play basketball.
___Betty's mom___ read a newspaper. ___She___ sat on a bench.

A

1. Ann walked to school with Jenny. A car splashed water on ~~her.~~ Ann.
2. Randy and Steve ran down the street. A black cat ran in front of ~~him.~~ Steve.
3. Tom saw Nancy at the store. The clerk was giving ~~Nancy~~ her change.
4. Frank talked to Peter. Everybody liked ~~him.~~ Peter.
5. Beth went swimming with Mike. She splashed water at ~~Mike.~~ him.

B

1. (He) went to the store after dinner.
2. (She) fell asleep before the movie ended.
3. (A bird) started to sing early in the morning.
4. (The boy) cleaned the garage after breakfast.
5. (Ann) fixed her car yesterday.
6. (All the people) clapped when the movie ended.

*See page 37 for Editing and Correcting a
Paragraph answers.

A

1. Don and Mark raked leaves. Carol gave ~~him~~ Don a bag for the leaves.
2. Mr. Swift fixed lunch for Miss Adams. He gave ~~her~~ Miss Adams a large bowl of soup.
3. Linda wanted to be a clown for Halloween. Steve found a funny outfit for ~~her~~ Linda to wear.
4. Tina and Alice waited in the doctor's office. The nurse told ~~her~~ Alice to go into the room.
5. Jeff and Kurt left school. Mr. Dukes gave ~~him~~ Kurt a ride home.

B

1. (Two trees) fell down during the storm.
2. (The baby) started to cry when his mother left the room.
3. (Tom) finished his homework at eleven o'clock in the morning.
4. (The boy) cleaned his room while his mother went shopping.
5. (They) shook hands after the game.
6. (We) went to the movies last night.

TEST 3

Test Score ☐

Lesson 30

A The number after each item tells how many mistakes in the item. Fix up the mistakes.

        T   went
1. the boys ~~good~~ to Bill's house. (3)
        S
2. Alice fell asleep. she was very tired. (2)
  T
3. that boy's shirt has six red buttons and four yellow buttons. (3)
          J G   A J
4. My best friends are jerry gomez and alex jordan. (4)
           R   R
5. Melissa and richard put their dog on richard's bed. (3)
6. We looked outside. ~~and~~ The rain had just stopped. (2)

B Fill in the blanks.

___Ann___ and ___Kim___ were swimming. ___Ann___ wore a bathing cap. ___She___ also wore a watch. ___Jane___ sat near the water. ___She___ wore sunglasses. ___Sally___ stood next to the blanket. ___She___ wore shorts. ___She___ read a book.

[illustration: Sally, Jane, Ann, Kim]

C Circle the subject in each sentence.
Write **P** in front of every sentence that has a pronoun for a subject.

___ 1. (Donald) planted corn.
_P_ 2. (It) had a broken handle.
_P_ 3. (He) kicked a football.
___ 4. (Betty) baked three pies.
___ 5. (The truck) had 16 wheels.
_P_ 6. (They) woke up late.
_P_ 7. (She) planted corn.
___ 8. (Bugs) ran all over the table.

D Put in an apostrophe if the words tell that the underlined object belongs to someone.

1. a girl's <u>hairbrush</u>
2. that cat's <u>tail</u>
3. the birds in the <u>tree</u>
4. the bugs on the <u>table</u>
5. an old man's <u>face</u>
6. the woman's <u>umbrella</u>
7. many <u>cups</u>
8. a girl's <u>suitcase</u>

Lesson 30 — Test 3 63   64 *Lesson 30 — Test 3*

Lesson 30

A

1. (He) brushed his teeth <u>after he washed his face.</u>
2. (James and Tom) did their math <u>in the morning.</u>
3. (The engine) made a funny noise <u>before the car stopped.</u>
4. (Tom) read a book <u>while he waited for his brother.</u>
5. (Alice and her mother) went shopping <u>yesterday afternoon.</u>
6. (Our teacher) read a story <u>during the lunch hour.</u>
7. (The clown) climbed the rope <u>when a bell rang.</u>
8. (Smoke) came from the house <u>after lightning hit it.</u>

B Write each sentence with the correct punctuation.
Make sure you follow these punctuation rules:
    a. Put a comma after the word **said.**
    b. Capitalize the first word the person said.
    c. Put a period or a question mark after the last word the person said.
    d. Put quote marks around the exact words the person said.

           "W
1. She said why are you so happy?"
        "T
2. He said the sun is shining."
          "D
3. Tim said do you have a pencil?"
           "M
4. Alice said my pencil is broken."

See page 43 for Editing and Correcting a Paragraph answers.

Lesson 31

A

1. (Our dog) barked <u>when the door opened.</u>
2. (We) went shopping <u>last night.</u>
3. (The girls) painted the room <u>while the boys washed the car.</u>
4. (Everybody) fell asleep <u>after lunch.</u>
5. (He) held his nose <u>as he jumped into the water.</u>
6. (Nobody) talked <u>during the movie.</u>

B Write **V** above each **verb.** Write **P** above each **pronoun.**

   P V
1. <u>It</u> <u>was landing</u> on the runway.
   1 2
    P   V   P
2. <u>They</u> wheeled <u>it</u> into the store.
    3   4
            V   P
3. The dog <u>barked</u> loudly at <u>him.</u>
           5   6
  P   V
4. <u>He</u> <u>forgot</u> his homework.
   7 8

Lesson 30 65   66 *Lesson 31*

16

Lesson 32

A

1. (John) went home after the party.
2. After the party, (John) went home.

3. (The girls) were tired by the time the sun went down.
4. By the time the sun went down, (the girls) were tired.

5. (The engine) made a funny noise before the car stopped.
6. Before the car stopped, (the engine) made a funny noise.

7. (Tammy) listened to the radio while Bill did his homework.
8. While Bill did his homework, (Tammy) listened to the radio.

B

1. Tom said, "~~w~~ W why did you do that?" (2)
2. They ~~seen~~ saw F Fred and J Jerry at the store. (3)
3. Maria said, "~~I~~ I love math." (2)
4. Lisa ~~teached~~ taught Mary's brother to swim. (2)
5. My sister went to the doctor, ~~and she~~ S she had a cold. (3)

*See page 41 for Editing and Correcting a Paragraph answers.

Lesson 33

A

Circle the subject.
Underline the whole predicate.
Make a line over the part that tells when.

1. (Jane) got a lot of work done while the baby slept.
   While the baby slept, (Jane) got a lot of work done.

2. (The birds) flew south in September.
   In September, (the birds) flew south.

3. (She) woke up before the alarm clock rang.
   Before the alarm clock rang, (she) woke up.

4. (He) worked on his boat every night.
   Every night, (he) worked on his boat.

B

1. The dogs chased the cats. I watched ~~them~~ the cats climb up a tree.

2. The boys and girls cleaned the house. ~~They~~ The boys washed the windows.

3. The rabbits ran under the fence. ~~The rabbits~~ They wanted the carrots.

2. Linda spoke to the boys. She told ~~the boys~~ them about the test.

5. He washed the forks and spoons. He put ~~them~~ the forks on the table.

Lesson 34

A

1. (Jane) walked home after school.
   After school, (Jane) walked home.

2. (Tom) read a book in the evening.
   In the evening, (Tom) read a book.

3. (The girl) rubbed her eyes when the lights came on.
   When the lights came on, (the girl) rubbed her eyes.

B

1. Sally had pencils and pens. She gave ~~them~~ the pens to her friend.

2. Tony found two kittens. He gave ~~the kittens~~ them some milk.

3. We saw bears and elephants. ~~They~~ The elephants were eating peanuts.

4. The boys and girls played baseball. ~~They~~ The girls won the game.

C

1. They said, "~~we~~ "W we are hungry." (4)
2. She ~~teached~~ taught Jerry to cook. (2)
3. I said "~~are~~ A are you tired?" (3)
4. The bus went up the hill. ~~It~~ I It made lots of noise. (2)
5. Jeff made dinner, ~~and he~~ H He made a pie for dessert. (4)

*See page 37 for Editing and Correcting a Paragraph answers.

Lesson 35

A

Write **N** above the noun in each subject.

1. Dark **N** clouds covered the sky.
2. An old **N** dog slept on the floor.
3. The **N** trucks got dirty.
4. Her little **N** bike cost a lot of money.
5. My **N** sister walked to school.

B

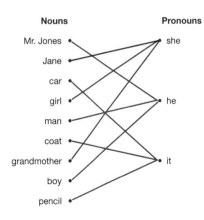

Nouns	Pronouns
Mr. Jones	she
Jane	
car	
girl	he
man	
coat	
grandmother	it
boy	
pencil	

17

A

girl — it
truck
Tom
apple — her
sister
uncle
Linda
light — him
boy

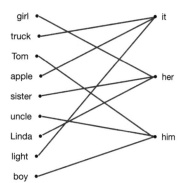

B

P 1. He fell asleep on the floor.
N 2. A big bird flew into the nest.
N 3. Alice came home early.
P 4. It made a big noise.
N 5. The young man started to speak.
N 6. Those girls are my sisters.

*See page 42 for Editing and Correcting a Paragraph answers.

A

P 1. A broken bottle was on the floor. (N above bottle)
P 2. It cost too much.
___ 3. She is older than her sister. (N above sister)
___ 4. That invention was very helpful. (N above invention)
P 5. Frogs make funny noises. (N above Frogs)
___ 6. They are sleeping.

B

1. James said, "Today is my birthday. We are having a party." (2)
2. Bill met Alice in the park. She said, "you look good." (4) (Y above you)
3. Ann's dad is very tall. He plays basketball. (3) (H above He)
4. The doctor said, "you have a bad cold. Don't go outside." (4) (Y above you)
5. I seen ann and jane at Mr. Jordan's house. (5) (saw A J J corrections)

A

Write **N** above each noun.
Write **P** above each pronoun.
Write **V** above each verb.

1. Six rabbits played on it. (N V P)
2. Tom looked at them. (N V P)
3. They talked to him after lunch. (P V P)
4. The meeting made her mad. (N V P)
5. She saw it when she came home. (P V P)
6. A big dog was with her. (N V P)

B   Put in the correct ending mark.

1. When did you go home?   5. That dog is mean.
2. You can go to the movies.   6. Can you come with us?
3. Did you find your hat?   7. Is your dog in the house?
4. My brother is sick.

C

1. He said, "I can't find my dog. Have you seen him?" (3)
2. She can drive a car and her brother taught her to drive. (3) (A C J)
3. Linda adams and chris jordan were in my class. (4) (A C J)
4. James said, "where is Tom's shirt? He wants it back." (3) (W)
5. My brother was sick. He had a bad cold. (2) (H)

*See page 43 for Editing and Correcting a Paragraph answers.

A

1. (The boys) went home after school.
2. During the rainstorm, (our dog) hid under the bed.
3. After we fixed the car, (we) made dinner.
4. In the morning, (Jane) walked to school.
5. (That girl) was happy when she got her report card.
6. (He) fell asleep while he read a book.
7. After James sat down, (the music) started.

B   Put in the correct ending mark.

1. Where is Tom?   5. A bird flew into the room.
2. Tom and Sally went home. 6. Is your brother here?
3. Did you see that bird?   7. She did not see her friend.
4. Can he eat that big hamburger?

C   Write **N** above each noun.
Write **P** above each pronoun.
Write **V** above each verb.

1. She stood next to him. (P V P)
2. That girl gave him a book. (N V P)
3. James saw her through that window. (N V P)
4. Our cat played with them. (N V P)
5. They were on top of it. (P V P)

TEST 4   Test Score [ ]

A
Write **N** above each noun.
Write **P** above each pronoun.
Write **V** above each verb.

1. That new boy sat next to him.
   (N above boy, V above sat, P above him)
2. Linda and her friend fixed it.
   (N above Linda, V above fixed, P above it)
3. She took them to the park.
   (P above She, V above took, P above them)
4. Six cows walked behind her.
   (N above cows, V above walked, P above her)

B
Rewrite each sentence so it begins with the part that tells when.

1. She fixed her car in the morning.

   <u>In the morning, she fixed her car.</u>

2. He went to sleep after he brushed his teeth.

   <u>After he brushed his teeth, he went to sleep.</u>

3. The baby woke up when the bell rang.

   <u>When the bell rang, the baby woke up.</u>

4. Nobody talked during the movie.

   <u>During the movie, nobody talked.</u>

C The number after each item tells how many mistakes are in the item. Fix up the mistakes.

1. Marias dog chased two cats up a tree. (2)
2. The babies fell asleep on Anns bed. (2)
3. Mr. adams said, "I liked that book." (3)
4. Ann met Lindas brother. he was very tall. (3)
5. He said, my team won the game. (4)

D For each picture, write the sentences that tell the exact words the person said.

1.

Hiro

2.

Heather

| 1. | Hiro said, "Can you help me? My dog is lost." |
| 2. | Heather said, "That was fun. I had a good time." |

A Put commas in the sentences that begin with the part that tells when.

1. (A cat) jumped up when the alarm clock rang.
2. When we got home, (the dog) started barking.
3. In the morning, (we) ate breakfast.
4. While the baby slept, (we) talked quietly.
5. (Her brother) was happy when he got the letter.
6. (They) finished the job just before midnight.
7. Before they made lunch, (the cooks) washed their hands.

B For each sentence, fill in the blank with the word **asked** or the word **said**. Then make the correct ending mark.

1. The girl _asked_, "Will you go with us?"
2. The girl _said_, "I want to go with you."
3. My friend _said_, "I love baseball."
4. My friend _asked_, "Do you like baseball?"
5. Ken _asked_, "Is it snowing?"
6. Ken _said_, "The snow is two feet deep."

C Write **N** in front of each noun.

1. N girl
2. N men
3. ___ they
4. ___ us
5. ___ yellow
6. N phone
7. ___ happy
8. ___ me
9. N mud

A
Write **N** above each noun.
Write **P** above each pronoun.
Write **V** above each verb.

1. They were on top of it.
   (P above They, V above were, P above it)
2. A big dog followed them up the hill.
   (N above dog, V above followed, P above them)
3. She gave him the ball.
   (P above She, V above gave, P above him)
4. Jerry was next to her.
   (N above Jerry, V above was, P above her)

B Write **N** in front of each noun.

1. N pen
2. ___ us
3. N flag
4. ___ under
5. N song
6. ___ them
7. ___ her
8. ___ found
9. N clouds
10. N school
11. N puppies
12. N party

C For each sentence, fill in the blank with the word **asked** or the word **said**. Then make the correct ending mark.

1. He _asked_, "Why are you so sad?"
2. She _said_, "He has my book."
3. His friend _asked_, "Where is the game?"
4. My sister _asked_, "Can we have a cookie?"

*See page 40 for Editing and Correcting a Paragraph answers.

19

A

    P   V   N
1. She bought a new car.
    P V   N
2. They went to a crowded beach.
   N   V   P
3. Sam cooked dinner for them.
     N V   P
4. My truck ran over it.

B For each sentence, fill in the blank with the word **asked** or the word **said.** Then make the correct ending mark.

1. He ___asked___ , "Is your brother home?"
2. He ___said___ , "We had a good time. "
3. She ___said___ , "My friend went home. "
4. She ___asked___ , "Where is the dog?"

C Copy the paragraph. Change three sentences so they begin with the part that tells when.

    Tom got up early in the morning. He ate breakfast after he put on warm clothes. Carol and her mother came over to Tom's house at 9 o'clock. They took Tom to a mountain. It was covered with snow. Tom and Carol threw snowballs when they got to the mountain top.

(Students copy paragraph on lined paper. Accept any 3 sentences transposed to begin with the part that tells when.)

A Punctuate the sentences that tell the exact words a person said. Put in the missing commas, quote marks and capital letters.

Jerry called Tom on the phone. Jerry asked Tom, "Can you go to the movies?"
Tom asked his mother, "Can I go to the movies?"
His mother said, "You can go when you finish your homework."
Tom finished his homework quickly. Tom's mom took Jerry and Tom to the movies later that day.

B Write **N** above each noun. Write **P** above each pronoun. Write **V** above each verb.

     N   V N   P
1. The wind blew water at them.
      N   V   N   P
2. My brother put salt on it.
  P   V   N   N
3. She wanted a new bike last summer.
        N V P P
4. That old man sold it to me.

C

1. At midnight, the dog began to bark. (2)
2. The streets flooded, during the rain storm. (2)
3. She bought a book, before the store closed. (2)
4. While the wind blew, everybody stayed inside Tom's house. (3)
5. Ann fell asleep while Tom's dad sang. (2)
6. Two old trees fell down, last night. (1)
7. Before Ann's dad made breakfast, we washed our hands. (2)

*See page 38 for Editing and Correcting a Paragraph answers.

A Write **N** above each noun. Write **P** above each pronoun. Write **V** above each verb.

  P   V P   N
1. He threw it at the wall.
   N   N   V   P
2. Tim and Donna were mad at them.
    N   N   V   P
3. The dogs and cats ran after me.
    N   V N   P
4. Her arm had a bug on it.

B Fix up any mistakes in each item.

1. When Alice got to school, nobody was there. (3)
2. Jerry asked his mother, "Can I stay home?" (3)
3. Tom asked his sister, "Where is my shirt?" (5)
4. My sister wasn't home. She went to Alice's house. (2)
5. As Mr. Jordan left, the children waved to him. (4)
6. Bill cleaned his room, before he ate breakfast. (2)

Lesson 46

A

Write **N** above each noun.
Write **P** above each pronoun.
Write **V** above each verb.

      N   N   V P
1. A girl and her dog chased it around the park.

  P V   N   N
2. He was between a little desk and a big table.

             P V N   N   N
3. Yesterday morning, she ate eggs and toast for breakfast.

      N   P V   P
4. In the morning, they took him to see me.

B

A.   B.   C.   D.

1. The boy was tall. _A, B, D_

2. The boy was tall. He wore shorts. _B, D_

3. The boy was tall. He wore shorts. He held a bat. _D_

*See page 42 for Editing and Correcting a
Paragraph answers.

Lesson 47

A

         N   V   N   N
1. Ted and Hilda were on the bank of a stream.

             N   V   N   V   N
2. When the sun came up, Ginger and Tom walked to the barn.

         N   N   V   P
3. Before school, the little boy looked for them.

  P V   N
4. She felt tired after the party.

B

Rule: If you remove the word **and,** you must replace it with a comma.

1. Ann had fun swimming,~~and~~ playing ball and digging in the sand.

2. Girls,~~and~~ boys,~~and~~ dogs and cats slid down the hill.

3. James read a book,~~and~~ wrote two letters,~~and~~ called his uncle and cleaned his room.

4. A cat,~~and~~ a dog,~~and~~ a pig and a horse ran into the barn.

C

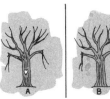 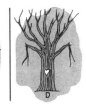

A   B   C   D

1. The tree was small. _A, B, C_

2. The tree was small. It had broken branches. _A, B_

3. The tree was small. It had broken branches. It had a heart carved on it. _A_

Lesson 48

A

     N   N   V   P
1. A dog and a cat were next to her.

          N   V   P   V   N
2. After the rain stopped, they went to his house.

 P V   N   N
3. She put apples and oranges in her bag.

         N   N   V   P
4. Yesterday morning, their mother drove them to school.

B

• If there are two **ands,** cross out the first **and.** Replace it with a comma.
• If there is only one **and,** leave it.

1. Tom ate chicken,~~and~~ peas and carrots.

2. Jane jumped rope,~~and~~ climbed on the bars and walked on her hands.

3. Jerry jumped up and ran to the door.

4. A book,~~and~~ a pencil and a cup fell off the table.

5. Alice opened the door,~~and~~ got into the car and drove to work.

6. James and his sister went home.

7. Jane,~~and~~ Tom and Bill ate lunch under the tree.

Lesson 48

C

A   B   C   D

1. The house had two trees next to it. It had broken windows. _B, D_

2. The house had two trees next to it. It had broken windows. It had a chimney. _B_

3. The house had two trees next to it. _A, B, D_

*See page 41 for Editing and Correcting a
Paragraph answers.

Lesson 49

A
- If there are two **ands**, cross out the first **and**. Replace it with a comma.
- If there is only one **and**, leave it.

1. Jerry got into the car, ~~and~~ turned on the engine and drove home.
2. Mary, ~~and~~ Jim and Tom were sick yesterday.
3. James ate a piece of bread and drank a glass of milk.
4. Bill wore black shoes, ~~and~~ a red shirt and brown pants.
5. A cat, ~~and~~ a dog and a pig lived in the barn.
6. My mother and my little sister walked to the store.
7. Walter washed the windows, ~~and~~ made his bed and swept the floor.

B Fix up any mistakes in each item.

1. Bill asked his mother, "when will we eat dinner?" (5)
2. When the dog barked at a cat, The baby woke up. (2)
3. Tom brushed his teeth, after he washed his face. (2)
4. Abdul said, "I am hungry. I want an apple." (2)
5. The boys cleaned their teachers' desk. (1)
6. Where is Mr. Suzuki? (3)

Lesson 50 — TEST 5

Lesson 50 TEST 5   Test Score [ ]

A
Write **N** above each noun.
Write **P** above each pronoun.
Write **V** above each verb.

1. My sister found them in her coat.
   N   V   P   N
2. In the morning, he wrote a letter.
   N   P   V   N
3. Yesterday afternoon, they saw a movie about Texas.
   P   V   N   N
4. She walked in the street with her dog.
   P V   N   N

B For each sentence, circle the subject and underline the whole predicate.

1. (My sister and I) went home on the bus.
2. After the sun went down, (the sky) became cloudy.
3. While the baby slept, (everybody) whispered.
4. (Those birds) will fly away when they finish eating.
5. In the evening, (James) read a book.

Lesson 50

C For each sentence, fill in the blank with the word **asked** or the word **said**. Then make the correct ending mark.

1. James __asked__, "Can you help me?"
2. They __said__, "We won the game."
3. She __said__, "My dog's name is Rover."
4. He __asked__, "What is your dog's name?"

D Put a comma in each sentence that begins with the part that tells when.

1. While the wind blew, everybody stayed inside.
2. My sister got home before I did.
3. After the rain stopped, my friends and I walked home.
4. As she walked home, Julie listened to the music.
5. An old tree fell down during the storm.
6. Before our dad made breakfast, we cleaned our room.
7. All the cars stopped when the light turned red.

*See page 43 for Editing and Correcting a Paragraph answers.

Lesson 51

A Complete each sentence with the verb **was** or the verb **were**.

1. Those girls __were__ happy.
2. Girls and boys __were__ hungry.
3. A baby __was__ sleepy.
4. Five dogs __were__ chasing a cat.
5. Those three books __were__ new.
6. My mother __was__ next to the car.
7. He __was__ at the park.
8. They __were__ late for school.

B
1. (She) had more stickers than James had.
   P   V   N
2. Yesterday afternoon, (they) cleaned their room.
   N   P   V   N
3. When the sun came up, (Alice) called him.
   N   N V P
4. (My sister) gave me a new shirt.
   N V P

C Fix up the sentences that have too many **ands**.

1. They bought three apples and six oranges.
2. His sister bought five apples, ~~and~~ two oranges and three carrots.
3. Raymond and Ned talked quietly.
4. Alice, ~~and~~ Julio and Clark talked quietly.
5. We cleaned our room, ~~and~~ ate dinner and did our homework before we went to sleep.

A Complete each sentence with the verb **was** or the verb **were**.

1. My father __was__ sick.
2. Her older brothers __were__ behind the car.
3. They __were__ eating dinner.
4. Two horses __were__ in the barn.
5. I __was__ walking my dog.
6. Their dad __was__ eating lunch.
7. My mother and father __were__ happy.

B

    N   P V   N
1. Last winter, (they) went to see their grandmother.
  P V   N
2. (It) was next to the big bottle.
        P   P   V   N
3. After they ate, (she) played with the baby.
  N   N   V   P
4. (Linda and James) sat near me.

C Use your lined paper. Rewrite each sentence so the word **and** appears only once.

1. The boy ran and slipped on the ice and fell down.
2. John and Mary and Jim went jogging.
3. They were tired and thirsty and hungry. *See page 38 for Editing and Correcting a Paragraph answers.

A Complete each sentence with the verb **was** or the verb **were**.

1. Jenny and John __were__ reading.
2. That pencil __was__ sharp.
3. Five fish __were__ swimming in the tank.
4. Terry __was__ fishing from the boat.
5. An old woman __was__ tired.
6. They __were__ playing football.

B Fix up any mistakes in each item.

                      W
1. Alice asked, "where is my car?" (3)
        M A
2. After mr. adams ate, he went home. (3)
                     "C
3. James asked his mother, "can I go out to play?" (3)
4. Alice sat down, when she finished the race. (1)
                   A ,
5. Two birds flew over anns head. (3)

A Complete each sentence with the verb **was** or the verb **were**.

1. You __were__ right.
2. You __were__ late yesterday.
3. She __was__ sad.
4. You __were__ not home yesterday.
5. He __was__ late.
6. They __were__ sick.
7. His dog __was__ friendly.
8. You __were__ hiding.

B I.

1. Write a description about picture 1. Tell where the women were and what they were doing.
2. Write a description about picture 2. Tell where the women were and what they were doing. *See page 42 for Editing and Correcting a Paragraph answers.

A

             N   V   P   N
1. Suddenly, (a big wind) knocked him off the chair.
     V   N   N   N
2. (He) put a cow and a pig in the old red barn.
         N   N   P   N
3. After lunch, (my mother) took me to the swimming pool.
     N   V   P
4. (A snowball) landed next to her.

B For each noun, write **day**, **month** or **name**.

1. Jay Turner __name__
2. October __month__
3. Wednesday __day__
4. Friday __day__
5. David __name__
6. December __month__

C

1. Make up a sentence that tells who **went into the store.**
2. Make up a sentence that tells which animals **stood on a diving board.**
3. Make up a sentence that tells the things **the woman juggled.**

*See page 43 for Editing and Correcting a Paragraph answers.

A

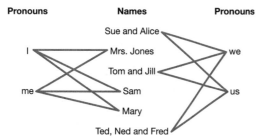

Pronouns	Names	Pronouns
	Sue and Alice	
I	Mrs. Jones	we
	Tom and Jill	
me	Sam	us
	Mary	
	Ted, Ned and Fred	

B

1. After the rain stopped, (we) walked to school.
   N — P V N
2. Last night, (I) helped him do his homework.
   P V P N
3. (The airplane) took her to Texas.
   N V P N
4. (She) taught me how to fix bikes.
   P V P N

A

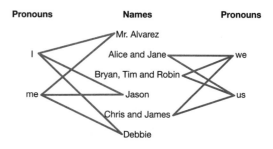

Pronouns	Names	Pronouns
	Mr. Alvarez	
I	Alice and Jane	we
	Bryan, Tim and Robin	
me	Jason	us
	Chris and James	
	Debbie	

B Fix up the mistakes in each item.

1. Tom and I was both born on the first wednesday in december. (3)
   were W D
2. Janes hand got dirty when she planted trees. (3)
   '
3. Ann visited her grandmother every monday night in april and may. (3)
   M A M
4. Cats and dogs was running in Toms yard. (2)
   were '
5. Alex and i were talking to cora. (2)
   I C
6. Kay asked her dad, can i stay up late? (5)
   "C I "
7. When mr. adams got home on Thursday, he read the newspaper. (4)
   M A h

*See page 39 for Editing and Correcting a Paragraph answers.

A

1. At last, (my brother and I) finished our homework.
   N P V N
2. Yesterday, (we) helped Mary fix her car.
   P V N N
3. (Alice and her sister) were not with me.
   N N V P
4. (Her car) had a racing stripe.
   N V N

B Fix up the mistakes in each item.

1. Mr. Adams and mrs. sanchez was sick on wednesday. (4)
   M S *were* W
2. Jill asked Tom, can i help you? (4)
   "C I
3. When my mom walked into the room, My baby sister smiled. (2)
   m
4. Where did you put Jills coat? (2)
   '
5. You was born in february. (2)
   were F
6. She asked, was he born in september or october? (5)
   "W S O "

A

1. After the rain stopped, (Alice and I) walked home.
   N P V N
2. (We) played basketball with a tall man.
   P V N N
3. (My friend) was next to me.
   N V P
4. After we ate lunch, (Bob) showed us how to fly kites.
   V N P N

B

1.

boxer

poodle   collie

2.

ax   Raymond

hammer

saw

1. Make up a sentence that tells who chased the squirrel.
2. Make up a sentence that tells what Raymond was holding.

Lesson 61

A

1. Last night, we ate dinner in a restaurant.
   P V   N
2. Her big sister was not with them.
  N   V   P
3. I called her this morning.
 P V   P   N
4. When the rain stopped, Liz and Alex walked home.
       N   N   N V

B

Rule: Any word that comes before the noun in the subject is an adjective.

1. A little puppy is barking.
      N
2. Nine boys ate lunch.
     N
3. A beautiful red kite flew in the air.
           N

C

For each sentence, circle the subject.
• Write **N** above the noun in the subject.
• Write **A** above each adjective in the subject.

1. An old tree grew next to the house.
  A A N
2. That farmer had big hands.
   A   N
3. Six little black cats ran in front of me.
  A   A   A   N
4. Small clouds moved across the sky.
   A   N
5. Those happy boys cheered loudly.
   A   A   N
6. The dog was hungry.
   A N

Lesson 61 99

Lesson 61

D Fix up the four unclear words in this passage.

One day, Tom and his dog went to the park with a Frisbee. The dog loved to play with the Frisbee and wagged its tail as they went to the park. As Tom and his dog played, ~~they~~ *two bear cubs* came out of the woods to watch.

Tom was pretending he was a star baseball player. He threw the Frisbee as hard as he could. It went over the dog's head and landed in the field. Tom and his dog ran after the Frisbee. ~~It~~ *A bear cub* grabbed the Frisbee.

As the dog barked at the bear cubs, ~~she~~ *the mother bear* came out from behind the trees. When Tom saw the mother bear, he grabbed ~~it~~ *his dog* and climbed up a tree.

100 *Lesson 61*

Lesson 62

A Fix up the four unclear words.

Ramon and Kevin worked at a rodeo. Kevin was a cowboy who rode bulls. ~~He~~ *Ramon* was a rodeo clown who helped cowboys.

One day, ~~he~~ *Kevin* tried to ride a fierce bull. He held on tightly as the bull jumped up and down. Suddenly, the bull turned sharply and threw Kevin to the ground. As Kevin sat on the ground holding his leg, ~~he~~ *Ramon* ran into the rodeo arena holding ~~it~~ *a barrel* over his head. Ramon put the barrel down on the ground and began to yell at the bull. The bull turned and ran toward the barrel. While Ramon helped Kevin walk away, the bull hit the barrel with its horns. Ramon had once again helped a cowboy who was in danger.

See page 39 for Editing and Correcting a Paragraph answers.

Lesson 62 101

Lesson 63

A Fix up the three unclear words in this passage.

Raymond loved to throw rocks. While Raymond was walking through the woods one day, he picked up some rocks and started throwing them at a tree. One rock missed the tree and hit ~~it~~ *a beehive*. ~~They~~ *The bees* were very mad. They flew out of the hive and headed straight toward Raymond. He ran away as quickly as he could. Just before the bees reached Raymond, he jumped into ~~it~~ *the pond*. He stayed in the pond until the bees returned to their nest.

102 *Lesson 63*

25

A

A N   A A N
1. His brother bought a new hat.

A N   A A N
2. My sister baked a yellow cake.

A A N   A A N
3. Five red ants climbed the kitchen wall.

A A A N   A A N
4. An old red cup fell off the big table.

B Fix up the mistakes in each sentence.

1. Jerry asked, "c̶an Raymond and i̶ go to the movies?" (4)
   C   I

2. My dads hand is twice as big as Jerrys hand. (2)
       '   '

3. When the baby fell asleep, e̶verybody was happy. (2)
                              E

4. Alice, Chuck and e̶llen ate lunch at Ellens house. (3)
                    E

5. December, j̶anuary and f̶ebruary was cold months. (4)
            J   F   were

6. Alice was very tired, when she got home on m̶onday. (2)
                                              M

*See page 44 for Editing and Correcting a
Paragraph answers.

A
- Write **N** above each noun.
- Write **A** above each adjective.

A N   A A N
1. One man held a big net.

A   N   A N
2. Her children bought ten cookies.

A A N   A A N
3. The gray squirrel climbed a tall tree.

A N   A A N
4. Two children washed their little dog.

B Cross out the letters of the sentences that are **not** relevant to the question.

How is wood used?

(a) Wood is used for building things. (b) Wood is also used for fuel.
(c) Some houses have walls that are made of wood. (d̶) Other houses are made
of brick. (e) The floors of many houses are made of wood. (f̶) Some houses
have floors made of concrete. (g̶) Concrete floors may crack when the house
gets old. (h) Some window frames are made of wood. (i) Fine tables and
chairs are made of wood. (j) Other chairs are made of metal or plastic.

C Fix up the three unclear words in this passage.

Early one morning, Tina drove her car to the garage where Robert, Sam
and Jane worked. After Tina parked her car in front of the gas pumps, h̶e̶
                                                            Robert
walked to the back of the car and opened the gas tank cover. As Robert put
            Sam   Jane
gas in the car, h̶e̶ cleaned the front windows. S̶h̶e̶ bent down and took a tire off
a car while the men worked on Tina's car.

A Write adjectives that make each subject complete.

1. _____ rabbit   3. _____ cup

2. _____ men   4. _____ monster

Accept reasonable answers.

B

                R V   N   N   N V   P
1. Suddenly he jumped out of bed.   Dan and his sister were with us.
      N   N V   N   N   P V   N
2. Nine men helped me fix my car.   After we ate, my mother was tired.

C The writer forgot to punctuate the sentences that tell the exact words
somebody said. Fix up those sentences.

> James did not do his homework last night.
>   "M
> He said, my teacher won't care. She likes me."
>
> James was wrong. His teacher did care. She
>   "Y
> said, you will stay in from recess to finish your
> work."
>
> James was not happy during recess. He
>   "T
> said, tonight I will finish my homework before I
> watch TV. I don't like missing recess."

*See page 40 for Editing and Correcting a
Paragraph answers.

A

Capitalize all parts of any item that names one person or one place.

1. that boy
2. $\underset{T}{\text{tom}}$
3. $\underset{M}{\text{mrs.}} \underset{R}{\text{robert}} \underset{B}{\text{brown}}$
4. my teacher
5. $\underset{L}{\text{lincoln}} \underset{S}{\text{street}}$
6. a repair shop

7. $\underset{J}{\text{johnson}} \underset{R}{\text{repair}} \underset{S}{\text{shop}}$
8. $\underset{C}{\text{chicago,}} \underset{I}{\text{illinois}}$
9. $\underset{M}{\text{mississippi}} \underset{R}{\text{river}}$
10. my store
11. $\underset{J}{\text{jolly}} \underset{T}{\text{time}} \underset{T}{\text{toy}} \underset{S}{\text{store}}$
12. that river

B

Cross out the letters of the sentences that are **not** relevant to the question.

What did Bob and Sally do when they saw a burning house?

(a) Bob and Sally ran into the house when they saw smoke coming from the house. (b) While Bob filled a pail with water, Sally grabbed the fire extinguisher. (c̶) Bob and Sally worked in the same factory. (d) They saw that a chair and a table were on fire. (e) Bob threw water on the chair while Sally squirted the fire extinguisher on the table. (f̶) That night, Bob and Sally watched television.

C

• Write **N** above each noun.
• Write **A** above each adjective.

1. $\underset{A}{\text{Three}} \underset{A}{\text{sad}} \underset{N}{\text{clowns}} \text{ rode a } \underset{A}{\text{tiny}} \underset{N}{\text{bicycle.}}$
2. $\underset{N}{\text{Kathy}} \text{ is sleeping on the } \underset{A}{\text{couch.}}$ (A N)
3. $\underset{A}{\text{A}} \underset{A}{\text{striped}} \underset{N}{\text{kite}} \text{ hit the } \underset{A}{\text{tree.}}$ (A N)
4. $\underset{A}{\text{A}} \underset{N}{\text{cow}} \text{ ate } \underset{N}{\text{grass.}}$

A

Capitalize all parts of any item that names one person or one place.

1. $\underset{U}{\text{uncle}} \underset{J}{\text{jake}}$
2. the street
3. $\underset{S}{\text{san}} \underset{F}{\text{francisco}}$
4. $\underset{K}{\text{kennedy}} \underset{H}{\text{high}} \underset{S}{\text{school}}$
5. our uncle
6. $\underset{A}{\text{ace}} \underset{T}{\text{toy}} \underset{F}{\text{factory}}$

7. $\underset{U}{\text{united}} \underset{S}{\text{states}}$
8. the mail carrier
9. $\underset{P}{\text{pacific}} \underset{O}{\text{ocean}}$
10. a big country
11. $\underset{J}{\text{japan}}$
12. $\underset{A}{\text{adams}} \underset{S}{\text{street}}$

B

• Write **N** above each noun.
• Write **A** above each adjective.

1. $\underset{A}{\text{His}} \underset{N}{\text{bear}} \text{ juggled } \underset{A}{\text{three}} \underset{N}{\text{balls.}}$
2. $\underset{A}{\text{A}} \underset{A}{\text{sick}} \underset{N}{\text{boy}} \text{ sat in a } \underset{A}{\text{wheelchair.}}$ (A N)
3. $\underset{N}{\text{Al}} \text{ ate } \underset{A}{\text{two}} \underset{N}{\text{apples.}}$
4. $\underset{A}{\text{That}} \underset{N}{\text{woman}} \text{ held a } \underset{A}{\text{small}} \underset{A}{\text{red}} \underset{N}{\text{purse.}}$
5. $\underset{A}{\text{Three}} \underset{N}{\text{people}} \text{ fixed } \underset{A}{\text{that}} \underset{A}{\text{old}} \underset{A}{\text{red}} \underset{N}{\text{car.}}$

C

Put the missing comma in each sentence that begins with a part that tells when.

As Wendy drove home from work, she thought of the banana pie that was in the refrigerator. Wendy was very hungry because she had not eaten lunch. After she parked her car, she ran into the kitchen and opened the refrigerator. Wendy could not believe her eyes. The refrigerator was empty. The banana pie was gone. Everything was gone. While Wendy was looking at the empty refrigerator, her brother walked into the kitchen. He looked nervous. After a few seconds, he walked up to his sister and said, "I'm sorry. I had some friends over for lunch and we ate all the food. Wait here. I'll be right back." Wendy sat down and waited. After a few minutes, her brother walked into the kitchen. He was carrying a bag filled with groceries. While Wendy took a nap, her brother cooked dinner. The dessert was a huge banana pie.

*See page 41 for Editing and Correcting a Paragraph answers.

A

Capitalize all parts of any item that names one person or one place.

1. $\underset{R}{\text{ruth}} \underset{G}{\text{garcia}}$
2. a doctor
3. a big building
4. $\underset{F}{\text{fairview}} \underset{H}{\text{hospital}}$

5. $\underset{D}{\text{don's}} \underset{S}{\text{supermarket}}$
6. $\underset{D}{\text{dr.}} \underset{B}{\text{brown}}$
7. that avenue
8. $\underset{S}{\text{salt}} \underset{L}{\text{lake}} \underset{C}{\text{city}}$

9. $\underset{M}{\text{mr.}} \underset{J}{\text{jordan}}$
10. his street
11. $\underset{F}{\text{florida}}$
12. $\underset{S}{\text{spring}} \underset{A}{\text{avenue}}$

B

1. $\underset{A}{\text{Seven}} \underset{N}{\text{men}} \text{ went to } \underset{V}{\text{went}} \underset{A}{\text{a}} \underset{A}{\text{big}} \underset{N}{\text{party.}}$
2. $\underset{A}{\text{Two}} \underset{A}{\text{little}} \underset{N}{\text{children}} \underset{V}{\text{stood}} \text{ in } \underset{A}{\text{deep}} \underset{N}{\text{snow.}}$
3. $\underset{N}{\text{James}} \underset{V}{\text{was}} \underset{V}{\text{wearing}} \underset{A}{\text{striped}} \underset{N}{\text{shorts.}}$
4. $\underset{A}{\text{An}} \underset{A}{\text{old}} \underset{N}{\text{woman}} \underset{V}{\text{gave}} \text{ me } \underset{A}{\text{a}} \underset{N}{\text{dollar.}}$

C

The writer forgot to punctuate the sentences that tell the exact words somebody said. Fix up those sentences.

	David walked up to his sister. He said, "I have a problem. My bike won't work."
	She said, "I will help you fix it." They worked for two hours. After they finished, the bike worked as well as ever.
	David said, "Thanks a lot. I really am happy that you are my sister."

TEST 7

Test Score [ ]

A Write **V** above each verb.
Write **N** above each noun.
Write **A** above each adjective.

   A A N V   A A N
1. Six new cars went up the steep hill.

  A A   N   V   A A N
2. A strong wind knocked over an old fence.

B Fix up each sentence so it is punctuated correctly.

1. Alice had a dog, a cat and a bird. (1)

2. Mr. James, Mrs. James and their son ate breakfast. (1)

3. We bought apples, oranges and pears at the store. (1)

C Capitalize all parts of any item that names one person or one place.

1. a big store

  U   S
2. united states

 D M
3. dr. mitchell

      C
4. california

    W   A
5. washington avenue

6. her house

7. that river

       A T S
8. ace toy store

D Fill in each blank with the verb **was** or **were**.

1. They ___were___ not home.

2. Jim's cat ___was___ sitting on the fence.

3. Anna and her mother ___were___ at the store.

4. You ___were___ right.

5. An old man ___was___ fishing.

6. You ___were___ not home last night.

*See page 38 for Editing and Correcting a Paragraph answers.

A For each item, write the sentence that answers the question.

1. Question: What are cheetahs?
Answer: The fastest land animals.
Cheetahs are the fastest land animals.

2. Question: Where do cheetahs live?
Answer: In Africa.
Cheetahs live in Africa.

3. Question: When do cheetahs hunt?
Answer: During the day.
Cheetahs hunt during the day.

4. Question: How fast do cheetahs run?
Answer: Over 60 miles an hour.
Cheetahs run over 60 miles an hour.

B

   A   N   V A   N
1. Five lions were in the cage.

 A   A   N   V   V
2. A small airplane is landing now.

     N   V   V   A   N
3. Steve was swimming in cold water.

    A A   N   V   A A N
4. The red ball bounced into a busy street.

C Put the missing comma in each sentence that begins with a part that tells when.

    Mr. Ross took his family out for dinner at a fancy restaurant. They had a very expensive meal. After they finished the meal, the waiter brought them the bill. Mr. Ross reached into his pocket for his wallet. As he reached into his pocket, he realized that he had left his wallet at home. He told the waiter about his problem. The waiter told the boss that Mr. Ross could not pay the bill. When the boss heard about the problem, she was not happy. The boss and Mr. Ross talked and came up with a solution to the problem. While his family went home to look for the wallet, Mr. Ross had to begin washing dishes. Mr. Ross put on an apron and began to wash the dishes. By the time his family came back with his wallet, Mr. Ross had washed all the dishes in the restaurant.

A For each item, write the sentence that answers the question.
(Students write sentences on lined paper.)

1. Question: Where do the largest elephants live?
Answer: In Africa.
The largest elephants live in Africa.

2. Question: How long do some elephants live?
Answer: More than 50 years.
Some elephants live more than 50 years.

3. Question: How much do some elephants weigh?
Answer: Up to six tons.
Some elephants weigh up to six tons.

B

        A N   P V A   N
1. When the bell rang, we went to our classroom.

    N   V   A A   N
2. Linda stood in front of a large desk.

  A   A A N   V   A   N
3. That tiny black fly flew into my cup.

      A   N A   A N   V
4. During the night, a strong wind blew.

*See page 44 for Editing and Correcting a Paragraph answers.

Lesson 73

A For each item, write the sentence that answers the question.

1. Question: Where do you find skunks?
   Answer: In North America.

You find skunks in North America.

2. Question: Why do skunks make a terrible smell?
   Answer: To defend themselves.

Skunks make a terrible smell to defend themselves.

3. Question: When do skunks usually sleep?
   Answer: During the daytime.

Skunks usually sleep during the daytime.

4. Question: How do skunks show that they are angry?
   Answer: By raising their tails.

Skunks show that they are angry by raising their tails.

B

        A A N P V   A A N
1. During the big storm, we went inside an old house.

   P V A A N A A N
2. He saw many black ants on the kitchen table.

  A A N V P
3. Two old men helped her.

  A N V   A A N
4. His truck moved slowly up a steep hill.

       A   N P V A N
5. After the meeting, she went to the store.

Lesson 74

A

  P V A A N   A A N
1. I found four red marbles under that old rug.

   A N P V N A N
2. Every day, we buy milk at the store.

  A   N   V   A A A N
3. An airplane flew over a big white cloud.

  A A N V   A A N
4. A bright light came from the third floor.

B

      M   R   U   S
1. The mississippi river is the longest river in the united states. (4)

      A   C
2. Texas alaska and california are the biggest states. (3)

    L A   S F
3. Is los angeles bigger than san francisco? (4)

         B   S
4. We lived on baldwin street until last september. (3)

                     S
5. After she brushed her teeth, she went to bed. (2)

               N Y D   M
6. My favorite cities are new york, dallas and miami. (5)

          M J   I
7. Ann asked mr. james, "Where can I buy that book?" (7)

*See page 39 for Editing and Correcting a Paragraph answers.

Lesson 75

A

1. Before the rain stopped.

(Sensible answer that includes "before the rain stopped.")

2. Stood on top of the table.

(Sensible answer that includes "stood on top of the table.")

3. She caught a bug.

(Sensible answer that includes "She caught a bug.")

4. Mary sat down.

(Sensible answer that includes "Mary sat down.")

5. Mary, Tom and their dog.

(Sensible answer that includes "Mary, Tom and their dog.")

6. After the show.

(Sensible answer that includes "after the show.")

B

     A N P V A N P N
1. After the storm, we had a fish in our basement.

  A   N   V P A A N
2. His mother told us a funny story.

   A N A   N   V V P
3. In my dream, five tigers were chasing me.

   N   N V   A N
4. Tom and Fran ran over that hill.

Lesson 76

A

1. After we finished eating.

(Sensible answer that includes "after we finished eating.")

2. He opened it.

3. A shirt, blue jeans and shoes.

(Sensible answer that includes "A shirt, blue jeans and shoes.")

4. Before the snow stopped.

(Sensible answer that includes "before the snow stopped.")

5. She jumped up.

B Write a good title sentence for each passage.

Passage 1

Laurie put on her swimming suit. She jumped into the pool. She swam across the pool three times. Then she got out of the pool and dried off.

(Idea: Laurie went swimming in a pool.)

Passage 2

Ted made his bed. He picked up his dirty clothes from the bedroom floor. He put things in his closet. He swept the floor of his room. Then he cleaned the windows in his room.

(Idea: Ted cleaned his bedroom.)

C Fix up the four unclear words in this passage.

James and Mike looked at the robot they had just built. The robot was

standing in the corner of the room holding a fishbowl over its head. ~~It~~ **Mike's dog** ran away

from the robot while the boys stood behind a big cardboard box.

"This is a disaster," ~~he~~ **James** said.

"I told you to be careful when you put the wires together," ~~he~~ **Mike** said.

The robot had already knocked over a lamp and broken a window. The

dog was terrified. ~~It~~ **The robot** said, "I must destroy. I must destroy."

*See page 40 for Editing and Correcting a
Paragraph answers.

A Write a good title sentence for each passage.

Passage 1

Kurt grabbed his dog and took it into the bathroom. He filled the bathtub with water. He put the dog in the tub. He rubbed soap on the dog. He rinsed off the dog.

(Idea: Kurt gave his dog a bath.)

Passage 2

Brad took a can of cat food from the shelf. He opened the can. He put the cat food in a small dish. Then he put the dish on the floor. His cat ate all the food.

(Idea: Brad fed his cat.)

B For each sentence, circle the subject and underline the predicate.
• Write **N** above each underlined noun.
• Write **A** above each underlined adjective.
• Write **V** above each underlined verb.
• Write **P** above each underlined pronoun.

1. Fran and Ray ran to the beach.

2. In the evening, I saw big spiders on our front steps.

3. That old car runs like a new car.

4. He slipped on the icy stairs.

A Write a good title sentence for each passage.

Passage 1

Steve took out some paper and a pen. He wrote on the paper. He put the paper in an envelope. He wrote his grandmother's name and address on the envelope. He put a stamp on the envelope.

(Idea: Steve wrote a letter to his grandmother.)

Passage 2

Melody put some paper in the fireplace. She put wood on top of the paper. She lit a match and held it under the paper. When the paper and wood started to burn, Melody closed the screen in front of the fireplace.

(Idea: Melody built a fire in the fireplace.)

B

1. The empire state building is in new york. (5)

2. Robert fed the dog, washed the dishes and cleaned his room before
   lunch. (1)

3. Is mexico larger than canada? (3)

4. Jill asked, "Where is Dr. Lee's office?" (2)

5. I bought apples, oranges and pears at the store. (1)

6. December, january and february are the coldest months of the year. (3)

7. Yoko's sister lives on washington street. (3)

8. Tom and his sister were in the park. (1)

*See page 38 for Editing and Correcting a
Paragraph answers.

A

1. Before we went to sleep.

(Sensible answer that includes "before we went to sleep.")

2. She helped him.

3. When they got home.

(Sensible answer that includes "when they got home.")

4. A truck, a car and a motorcycle.

(Sensible answer that includes "a truck, a car and a motorcycle.")

5. He stopped talking.

B For each sentence, circle the subject and underline the predicate.
• Write **N** above each underlined noun.
• Write **A** above each underlined adjective.
• Write **V** above each underlined verb.
• Write **P** above each underlined pronoun.

1. A large red truck stopped in front of them.

2. After school, six boys and two girls played in the gym.

3. She helped him fix the flat tire on his new bike.

TEST 8

Test Score ☐

A

```
      A    N  A   A  N V   N    P N
1. In the morning, my older sister fixed breakfast for our family.
   A A N  V     A A N
2. That old car stopped in front of a large building.
    P  V  V    P   V    A A  N
3. She was smiling when they went out the back door.
   A  A A N  V  V    A A   N
4. Two mean dogs were running after a yellow cat.
```

B

1. When she got home, everybody was sleeping. (1)
          M   A'
2. I live on madison avenue. (2)
       M   R   U   S
3. The mississippi river is the longest river in the united states. (4)
4. Renee asked Alfred, "Have you seen my brother? He has my pen." (1)
                              S F   G
5. Bills favorite team is the san francisco giants. (4)
       J   A
6. June, July and august are the warmest months. (3)
      D S   W   S ?
7. Does dr. spangler have an office on washington street ? (5)

A   Fix up the five unclear words in this passage.

An alligator
Just after the school bell rang, a strange thing happened. ~~It~~ walked into
The teacher
the classroom on its hind legs. The students couldn't believe their eyes. ~~She~~
was making marks on a piece of paper and didn't see the strange animal. The
alligator walked toward a seat next to a girl named Ann. "Why is everybody
the teacher
looking at the door?" ~~she~~ asked.
Kevin
"The new student has arrived," ~~he~~ said.
Ann
"Can the new student sit next to me?" ~~she~~ asked. She clapped her hands
as she thought about the strange things that might happen that day.

*See page 41 for Editing and Correcting a
Paragraph answers.

A   Use Reading Textbook B to answer these questions.

1. What part of your textbook shows a list of the selections in the book,
   starting with page 1? **The table of contents**

2. What is the title of the selection for lesson 134?
   A Book About the Poles

3. On what page does the selection for lesson 134 begin? **323**

4. What is the title of the selection for lesson 99? **End of the Race**

5. On what page does that selection begin? **143**

B

1. Write the date for the fifth day of August in the year 1968.
   August 5, 1968

2. Write the date for the third day of June in the year 2001.
   June 3, 2001

3. Write the date for the eleventh day of March in the year 1792.
   March 11, 1792

4. Write the date for the eighth day of July in the year 1812.
   July 8, 1812

5. Write the date for the nineteenth day of November in the year 1947.
   November 19, 1947

A   Use the table of contents in Reading Textbook B to answer these
         questions.

1. How many selections are listed for lesson 79? **2**

2. What's the title of the information passage? **Colorado and Utah**

3. What's the title of the story for lesson 79? **A Great Show**

4. On what page does the story for lesson 79 begin? **43**

5. What's the title for the selection that begins on page 138?
   Beware of Streams

B

1. Write the date for the 21st day of May in the year 1886.
   May 21, 1886

2. Write the date for the seventeenth day of September in the year 2010.
   September 17, 2010

3. Write the date for the tenth day of January in the year 1935.
   January 10, 1935

4. Write the date for the 23rd day of March in the year 1722.
   March 23, 1722

C

great	carrot	top	horse	right
visit	elephant	north	jail	millions

Lesson 83

A Use the table of contents in Reading Textbook B to answer these questions.

1. How many selections are listed for lesson 126? __2__
2. What's the page number for the first selection in lesson 126? __277__
3. What's the page number for the second selection in lesson 126? __278__
4. What's the title of the second selection? __Angela and Al Learn About the Eye.__

B

1. Greenville Iowa __Greenville, Iowa__
2. Street number: 45
   Street name: Vine Street
   City name: Greenville
   State name: Iowa
   Write the address with commas.
   __45 Vine Street, Greenville, Iowa__
3. Street number: 7
   Street name: Old Goat Road
   City name: Chico
   State name: California
   Write the address with commas.
   __7 Old Goat Road, Chico, California__

C

length	bedroom	globe	yellow	desk
raise	should	forest	umbrella	whole

   Lesson 83   **127**

Lesson 85

A

1. arrange __disarrange__
2. join __rejoin__
3. appear __reappear__
4. charge __discharge__

B Write **jump** or **jumps** in each sentence. Write **one** or **more than one** after each sentence.

1. The girl __jumps__. __one__
2. You and I __jump__. __more than one__
3. Cats and dogs __jump__. __more than one__
4. Those frogs __jump__. __more than one__
5. A man __jumps__. __one__
6. Mark and Henry __jump__. __more than one__

C Use the words below to make an alphabetical list.

higher	unless
tongue	funny
ocean	question
yourself	normal
insect	knocked

128   Lesson 85

Lesson 86

A Write **run** or **runs** in each sentence. Write **one** or **more than one** after each sentence.

1. This woman __runs__. __one__
2. Boys and girls __run__. __more than one__
3. She __runs__. __one__
4. Her pals __run__. __more than one__
5. Her pal __runs__. __one__
6. Two men __run__. __more than one__

B

	1	2	3
1.	approve	disapprove	reapprove
2.	arrange	rearrange	disarrange
3.	order	reorder	disorder
4.	join	disjoin	rejoin
5.	connect	disconnect	reconnect

C Use the words below to make an alphabetical list.

kitten	dance
officer	lifeboat
argued	half

    Lesson 86   **129**

Lesson 87

A Use the table of contents in Reading Textbook B to answer these questions.

1. What's the lesson number for the selection that begins on page 303? __131__
2. What's the title of the selection that begins on page 303?
   __Winter at the North Pole.__
3. What's the lesson number for the selection that begins on page 91? __89__
4. What's the title of the selection that begins on page 91?
   __Facts About the Iditarod.__

B

	1	2	3
1.	join	disjoin	rejoin
2.	order	reorder	disorder
3.	charge	discharge	recharge
4.	connect	reconnect	disconnect
5.	continue	recontinue	discontinue

C Write **hop** or **hops** in each sentence. Write **one** or **more than one** after each sentence.

1. Joan and Barry __hop__ over logs. __more than one__
2. She __hops__ over logs. __one__
3. They __hop__ over logs. __more than one__
4. This thin man __hops__ over logs. __one__

130   Lesson 87

A Write **sing** or **sings** in each sentence. Write **one** or **more than one** after each sentence.

1. His dad ___sings___ well. ___one___
2. His dad and mom ___sing___ well. ___more than one___
3. Those ten kids ___sing___ well. ___more than one___
4. Her older brothers ___sing___ well. ___more than one___

A Write **talk** or **talks** in each sentence. Write **one** or **more than one** after each sentence.

1. She ___talks___ fast. ___one___
2. That man ___talks___ fast. ___one___
3. Alvin and his brother ___talk___ fast. ___more than one___
4. Six parrots ___talk___ fast. ___more than one___

A

coat	mirror	1. ___machine___
climb	myna	2. ___metal___
canned	metal	3. ___mirror___
curly	money	4. ___money___
crazy	machine	5. ___myna___

B Write the word for each description.

1. What word means **without effort**? ___effortless___
2. What word means **without a home**? ___homeless___
3. What word means **to connect again**? ___reconnect___
4. What word means **the opposite of connect**? ___disconnect___
5. What word means **not zipped**? ___unzipped___
6. What word means **without a hat**? ___hatless___

A Write the first page of Reading Textbook B that tells about each topic.

1. blizzard ___132___
2. lungs ___254___
3. universe ___239___
4. Jupiter ___209___

B Underline the second letter in each word. Then write the words in alphabetical order.

squirrel   solid
steady   smelly
scale   shelves

1. ___scale___
2. ___shelves___
3. ___smelly___
4. ___solid___
5. ___squirrel___
6. ___steady___

C Write **run** or **runs** in each sentence. Write **one** or **more than one** after each sentence.

1. Those cars ___run___ on batteries. ___more than one___
2. That river ___runs___ to the sea. ___one___
3. Dogs ___run___ faster than people. ___more than one___
4. This man ___runs___ every day. ___one___

D Write the word for each description.

1. What word means **full of thought**? ___thoughtful___
2. What word means **the opposite of charged**? ___discharged___
3. What word means **without roads**? ___roadless___
4. What word means **to think again**? ___rethink___
5. What word means **without care**? ___careless___
6. What word means **full of care**? ___careful___

A Use Reading Textbook B to answer these questions.

1. You want to find the first page in the Reading Textbook that tells about computers. On what page does that topic begin? ___336___

2. Write the first word on that page. ___the___

3. What is the last page on which the topic **computer** appears? ___337___

4. Write the last word on that page. ___read___

5. You want to find the first page in the textbook that tells about **elephants.** On what page does that topic begin? ___210___

6. Write the first word on that page. ___suddenly___

7. What is the last page on which the topic **elephant** appears? ___231___

8. Write the last word on that page. ___old___

B Write **like** or **likes** in each sentence. Write **one** or **more than one** after each sentence.

1. His dad ___likes___ golf.   ___one___

2. Her parents ___like___ to dance.   ___more than one___

3. Kittens ___like___ milk.   ___more than one___

4. Our teacher ___likes___ to swim.   ___one___

C All the words in the box below begin with the letter **E**. Underline the second letter in each word. Then write the words in alphabetical order.

eraser   enormous   edge   easy   evening   escape   eggs   eyes

A Use Reading Textbook B to answer these questions.

1. You want to find the first page in the Reading Textbook that tells about the topic **biceps.** On what page does that topic begin? ___244___

2. Write the first word on that page. ___They___

3. What is the last page on which the topic **biceps** appears? ___245___

4. Write the last word on that page. ___neck___

5. You want to find the first page in the textbook that tells about the topic **jungle.** On what page does that topic begin? ___210___

6. Write the first word on that page. ___suddenly___

7. What is the last page on which the topic **jungle** appears? ___347___

8. Write the last word on that page. ___reading___

B Write **feel** or **feels** in each sentence. Write **one** or **more than one** after each sentence.

1. She ___feels___ sick.   ___one___

2. His forehead ___feels___ hot.   ___one___

3. These slippers ___feel___ like silk.   ___more than one___

4. We ___feel___ angry about the test.   ___more than one___

5. This bed ___feels___ too hard.   ___one___

6. They ___feel___ shy about singing.   ___more than one___

7. My feet ___feel___ sore.   ___more than one___

A

1. Jim ran very fast, but Linda ran even ___faster___.

2. All of the turtles are slow, but Amy's turtle is the ___slowest___.

3. Jan said to Al, "Let's go to the store." So Jan and Al ___went to the store___

4. There was a man in the room. Then another man walked into the room. So now there are two ___men (in the room)___

5. When I put my left foot in the tub, I had one wet foot. Then I put my right foot in the tub. So now I have two ___wet feet___.

6. The more you cut a moop's hair, the faster its hair grows. Bob kept cutting his moop's hair, so that moop's hair ___grew fast or grew faster___

B Use Reading Textbook B to answer these questions.

1. What part of the textbook gives an alphabetical listing of topics that appear in the book? ___index___

2. On what page does the topic **ocean** first appear in the textbook? ___139___

3. Write the first word on that page. ___couldn't___

4. What's the last page on which the topic **ocean** appears? ___347___

5. Write the last word on that page. ___reading___

C

change   cabbage   dollar   coast   decide   dream   circus

A Write the missing part in each item.

1. Last week Ted lost a tooth. This week the same thing happened. So now Ted has two missing ___teeth___.

2. At first one child was in the sandbox. Then another child came into the sandbox. Now there are ___two children___ in the sandbox.

3. We have had some hot days this summer, but today is the ___hottest___ day I can remember.

4. Jim said, "I will draw two pictures this week." And that is just what he did. He ___drew___ two pictures.

5. In school, there were three turtles. Ed's turtle was four years old. Greg's turtle was five years old, so it was one year ___older___ than Ed's turtle. Bonnie's turtle was 14 years old, so it was the ___oldest___ turtle in school.

6. Joe told his mom he would sweep the sidewalk. He started to sweep the sidewalk. When his sister asked him, "What are you doing?" Joe said, "I ___am sweeping (the sidewalk)___."

7. Henry had a loud voice. Tim spoke even ___louder___ than Henry. Ernie spoke the ___loudest___ of all.

B

thought   ruler   tenth   rich   taste   rough   return

Lesson 98

A

middle   (island)   m<u>a</u>chine   (insist)   m<u>u</u>mmy   m<u>o</u>ney   (idea)

1. _____idea_____
2. _____insist_____
3. _____island_____
4. _____machine_____
5. _____middle_____
6. _____money_____
7. _____mummy_____

Lesson 99

A

(flower)   juggle   (football)   (fence)   (fifty)   join

1. _____fence_____
2. _____fifty_____
3. _____flower_____
4. _____football_____
5. _____join_____
6. _____juggle_____

Lesson 98–99   **139**

Lesson 101

A   Draw a line from each expression to what it means.

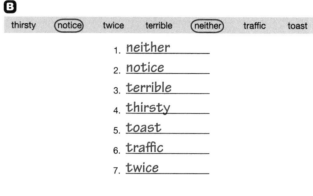

1. She slept like a log last night.
2. She was really hard-nosed.
3. Well, I'll be a monkey's uncle.
4. She talked until she was blue in the face.

- She was tough.
- She talked a lot.
- She slept very soundly.
- The person was really surprised.

B

thirsty   (notice)   twice   terrible   (neither)   traffic   toast

1. <u>neither</u>
2. <u>notice</u>
3. <u>terrible</u>
4. <u>thirsty</u>
5. <u>toast</u>
6. <u>traffic</u>
7. <u>twice</u>

140   Lesson 101

Lesson 102

A

1. **clothing**
   A. (name of a piece of clothing) _____
   B. (another piece of clothing) _____
   C. (another piece of clothing) _____

2. **tools**
   A. (name of a tool) _____
   B. (another tool) _____
   C. (another tool) _____

3. **vehicles**
   A. (name of a vehicle) _____
   B. (another vehicle) _____
   C. (another vehicle) _____

Lesson 102   **141**

Lesson 102

B   Draw a line from each expression to what it means.

1. He was always walking on thin ice.
2. It was raining cats and dogs.
3. He was really hard-nosed.
4. He could have been knocked over by a feather.
5. He slept like a log.
6. He always does best when his back is against the wall.

- He was tough.
- He was really surprised.
- He slept very soundly.
- He does best when he faces serious problems.
- He was always doing dangerous things.
- It was raining very hard.

142   Lesson 102

35

Lesson 103

A

| ruler | airplane | done | knives | thumb |
| dinner | ceiling | report | honest | weather |

1. **airplane**
2. **ceiling**
3. **dinner**
4. **done**
5. **honest**
6. **knives**
7. **report**
8. **ruler**
9. **thumb**
10. **weather**

B

1. fruits
   - A. (name of a fruit)
   - B. (name of another fruit)
   - C. (name of another fruit)
   - D. (name of another fruit)

2. vegetables
   - A. (name of a vegetable)
   - B. (name of another vegetable)
   - C. (name of another vegetable)
   - D. (name of another vegetable)

3. animals
   - A. (name of an animal)
   - B. (name of another animal)
   - C. (name of another animal)
   - D. (name of another animal)

Lesson 105

A

| shadow | lemon | giant | visit | destroy |
| great | younger | bread | space | globe |

B

THINGS I DID

_____ day _____ day _____ day

1. Day of week _____
   - A. (a thing student did on that day)
   - B. (another thing student did on that day)
   - C. (another thing student did on that day)
   - D. (another thing student did on that day)

2. Day of week _____
   - A. (a thing student did on that day)
   - B. (another thing student did on that day)
   - C. (another thing student did on that day)
   - D. (another thing student did on that day)

3. Day of week _____
   - A. (a thing student did on that day)
   - B. (another thing student did on that day)
   - C. (another thing student did on that day)
   - D. (another thing student did on that day)

Lesson 113

A

face	fasten
favorite	field
figure	first
five	float
foam	freeze
friend	frost

1. frond — **friend, frost**
2. fever — **favorite, field**
3. famous — **face, fasten**
4. flea — **five, float**
5. factory — **face, fasten**
6. finally — **figure, first**
7. forest — **foam, freeze**
8. faint — **face, fasten**
9. frisky — **friend, frost**
10. finish — **figure, first**

Lesson 114

A

label	lawyer
lazy	lifeboat
lightning	living
loaf	maggot
magic	matter
mean	meter

1. metal — **mean, meter**
2. list — **lightning, living**
3. ledge — **lazy, lifeboat**
4. machine — **loaf, maggot**
5. lady — **label, lawyer**
6. manage — **magic, matter**

A Write the name of the part of the book you would use for each item. The answer to each item is **glossary**, **index**, or **table of contents**.

1. You want to find out the page number for the first selection on lesson 71.
   table of contents

2. You want to find out what the word **image** means.
   glossary

3. You want to find out how many selections are presented in lesson 104.
   table of contents

B Use your dictionary to find the correct meaning of the underlined word in each sentence. Circle the correct meaning.

1. His story about what happened was <u>sincere</u>.
   • not true   (• honest)   • funny

2. She <u>ignited</u> the pile of tree branches.
   • collected   • cut up   (• set fire to)

C For each word, underline the prefix. Circle the root. Make a line over the suffix.

1. re(mark)able   2. dis(honest)ly

D

• Her cheeks were apples.

1. What two things are the same. _her cheeks and apples_

2. How are they the same? _Idea: They were both red._

E

1. The first speech was <u>brief</u>. The second speech was not very long either.
   short
2. Gina's dress had <u>vivid colors</u>, but her mother's was not very colorful.
   bright
3. The new <u>regulation</u> did not fit in with the other rules.
   rule

Draw a line from each word in the first column to the word that means the same thing.

1. brief •   • bright
2. vivid •   • rule
3. regulation •   • short

DID	The trail bike ~~crash~~ **crashed** into the tree. Fred
	fell off the bike. The big noise scared
WH	the bull. Rita saw that Fred was in
WH RO	trouble. The horse galloped toward Fred.
	~~and the~~ horse reached him just before the
	bull did.
	Idea: The bull charged toward Fred.
	Idea: She got on her horse.

Check 1: Did you write sentences that give a clear picture of what must have happened in the middle picture? (WH)
Check 2: Are all your sentences written correctly? (CP, DID, RO)

	The painter carried his ladder over to
RO	the tree ~~and~~ he leaned the ladder against
WH	the tree Mike picked some apples.
DID	He ~~toss~~ **tossed** the apples to the painter. The
CP	painter put the apples on the ground Anita
	unfolded the blanket. She took the food
	and drinks from the picnic basket and set
	them on the blanket.
	Idea: Mike climbed the ladder.

Check 1: Did you write sentences that give a clear picture of what must have happened in the middle picture? (WH)
Check 2: Are all your sentences written correctly? (CP, DID, RO)

	The back wheel of Alicia's bike was badly
	bent. Alicia took her bike to a bike repair
RO	shop. ~~and~~ the repair person looked at the
Q	bent wheel on her bike. He said, "I can fix
	that bike in five minutes." He put the bike
WH	on the counter. Alicia sat on a bench. She
	read a book and drank a soda while she
DID	waited. The bike repair person ~~work~~ worked on the
	bike for hours. He was not able to figure
	out how to fix the wheel.

Idea: He took the back wheel off the bike.

Check 1: Did you give a clear picture of what happened in the first picture? (WH)

Check 2: Did you correctly punctuate the sentence that tells what somebody said? (Q)

Check 3: Did you give a clear picture of what must have happened in the middle picture? (WH)

Check 4: Are all your sentences written correctly? (CP, RO, DID)

151

	Roger was looking for monkeys in the jungle. He
	caught a mother monkey. After he brought the
COM	monkey to his campsite, he locked it in a cage. He
	put the key to the cage on a table. He walked over
	to his cot and sat down. He said, "I finally caught
	that monkey. I'll take her back to the zoo." A baby
	monkey sat on a branch and watched what was
	happening.
	Roger took off his boots and laid down on the
	on the cot in his tent. The baby monkey climbed
	down the tree when Roger went to sleep. The baby
	monkey walked quietly to the table as Roger slept.
	The baby monkey took the key and opened the
	lock on the cage. The mother monkey walked out
	of the cage door after the baby monkey unlocked
	the cage. The monkeys grabbed some bananas
	from the table and climbed back up in the tree. Roger
	continued to sleep as the happy monkeys ate the
	bananas.
W-1	A sentence that begins with a part that tells when

Check 1: Does your first paragraph give a clear picture of what happened before the first picture and in the first picture? (WH)

Check 2: Does your second paragraph give a clear picture of what happened in the middle picture and the last picture? (WH, P)

Check 3: Did you write at least two sentences that begin with a part that tells when? (W, COM)

152

	The sheriff and his deputy were near the
	edge of an old wooden bridge that went
	across a stream. The sheriff was pointing
	across the stream. The deputy was
	standing behind the sheriff. The sheriff
DID	~~start~~ started to walk across the bridge. As the
	sheriff walked across the bridge, the
	deputy said, "That bridge doesn't seem
Q	safe." After the sheriff had taken a couple
	of steps, the bridge broke. The sheriff
	tumbled into the water. As the sheriff
COM	climbed out of the water, the deputy
	laughed and held out his hand to help the
	sheriff.

Check 1: Do your sentences about picture 1 tell where the sheriff and his deputy were and what they were doing? (WH)

Check 2: Do your sentences for the other pictures tell what somebody or something did? (WH, DID)

Check 3: Do you have at least one sentence that begins with a part that tells when? (W, COM)

153

	Sandra decided to take her dog ice
RO	skating at the pond. ~~and she~~ She rode her
	horse to the pond. Her dog followed the
	horse. When they got to the pond, Sandra
DID	~~climb~~ climbed off her horse and tied the reins to
	a nearby tree. She took off her coat and
WH	boots. Then she put four little skates on
	her dog. She picked up her dog and carried
	it through the snow to the ice.

Idea: She put on her ice skates.

Check 1: Did you give a clear picture of what happened in the first picture? (WH)

Check 2: Did you give a clear picture of what must have happened in the middle picture? (WH)

Check 3: Are all your sentences written correctly? (CP, DID, RO)

154

	Dave was working at an auto repair
CP	shop. _Hhe was changing a wheel. He told the
	woman he was working with, "After work, I
P	am going to the beach and cool off. _PWhen
	Dave finished work, he rode to the beach on
	his bike. His dog ran next to the bike. When
	he got to the beach, Dave changed into his
	swimsuit. He put his uniform and shoes
	next to his bike. He took the leash off his
	dog and ran through the sand into the
DID	water. His dog ~~follow~~ followed him. They went
	swimming. As Dave and his dog ran through
	the water, Dave said, "I love to go
Q	swimming on a hot day."

Check 1: Does your first paragraph give a clear picture of what happened in the first picture? (WH)

Check 2: Does your second paragraph give a clear picture of what happened in the middle picture and the last picture? (WH, P)

Check 3: Are all your sentences written correctly? (CP, RO, DID, Q)

155

DID	The elephant trainer ~~drive~~ drove the truck to
WH	the side of the road. The elephants
	walked out of the truck. The elephant
	trainer led the elephants across the road.
	John took the spare tire out of the car
RO	trunk. ~~and the~~ The elephants stood behind the
WH	car. John took the flat tire off the car
	and put it on the ground. He got ready to
	put the spare tire on the back wheel.
	Idea: The elephant trainer put down the ramp.
	Idea: The elephants lifted up the back of the car with their tusks.

Check 1: Did you write sentences that give a clear picture of what must have happened in the middle picture? (WH)

Check 2: Are all your sentences written correctly? (CP, DID, RO)

156

	Ron's boat sank near a desert island.
	Ron picked up his toolbox from the boat
CP	and stepped into the water. He said,
Q	"I'll need these tools." He walked through
	the water to the beach. He opened up the
WH	toolbox and took out an ax. He used the
	tree trunks to spell the word help on the
	beach. He also used the tree trunks and
RO	some leaves to build a shelter. ~~and~~ _Hhe sat
	and waited for help.
	Idea: He chopped down several trees.

Check 1: Did you give a clear picture of what happened in the first picture? (WH)

Check 2: Did you correctly punctuate the sentence that tells what somebody said? (Q)

Check 3: Did you give a clear picture of what must have happened in the middle picture? (WH)

Check 4: Are all your sentences written correctly? (CP, RO, DID)

157

	Mrs. Hart was walking down a hill with
CP	her dog. _Hher dog was walking behind her.
	Suddenly, Mrs. Hart tripped over a rock.
DID	Her dog stopped and ~~watch~~ watched her. Mrs.
	Hart rolled down the hill towards a cliff.
	When her dog saw that Mrs. Hart was in
COM	trouble, the dog started to run after her.
	Mrs. Hart rolled to the edge of the cliff.
	Just before she rolled over the edge of the
	cliff, her dog grabbed Mrs. Hart's coat and
	held onto her.

Check 1: Does your first paragraph give a clear picture of what happened before the first picture and in the first picture? (WH)

Check 2: Does your second paragraph give a clear picture of what happened in the missing picture and the last picture? (WH, P)

Check 3: Did you write at least two sentences that begin with a part that tells when? (W, COM)

158

39

	Tony and Rita were driving down the road
	in their truck when they came to a
	tunnel. The truck was too tall to get
RO	through the tunnel. ~~and~~ Tony and Rita got
DID	out of the truck. Tony ~~took~~ looked at the tunnel.
	He said, "How can we get through this
	tunnel?" Rita bent down next to the front tire.
	As Rita looked at the front tire, she
	got an idea. She told Tony that if they let
	some air out of the tires, the truck could
	be low enough to make it through the
	tunnel. They let air out of all the tires.
CP	Then, they drove slowly through the tunnel.
	the top of the truck was just low enough
WH	to get through the tunnel.

Idea: Tony said, "We made it through the tunnel. I hope that our tires are still good."

Check 1: Does your first paragraph give a clear picture of what happened before the first picture and in the first picture? (WH)

Check 2: Does your second paragraph give a clear picture of what happened in the middle picture and the last picture? (WH, P)

Check 3: Are all your sentences written correctly? (CP, RO, DID, Q)

159

	Mr. Wingate swung the net at the
RO	butterfly ~~and~~ the net missed the
WH	butterfly. The mother bear growled. Mr.
	Wingate heard the growl. He ran away as
CP	fast as he could. he ran towards a big tree.
	The mother bear ran after Mr. Wingate. He
DID	~~climb~~ climbed up the tree.

Idea: The net went over the head of the mother bear.

Check 1: Did you write sentences that give a clear picture of what must have happened in the middle picture? (WH)

Check 2: Are all your sentences written correctly? (CP, DID, RO)

160

	Henry and Carlos decided to go fishing
	on Saturday. Their alarm clock rang at
CP	6 in the morning. the boys sat up. Carlos
	reached to turn off the alarm clock. After
	a couple of minutes, the boys got out of
WH	bed. They put the boat on the trailer and
	drove to the lake. When they arrived at the
	lake, they took the boat off the trailer and
	carried it into the water. Both boys put on
	their life jackets and got ready to go
	fishing. Carlos carried the oars into the
DID	boat and ~~climb~~ climbed onto the front seat. Henry
	sat in the back seat with the fishing pole.

Idea: They got dressed and went outside.

Check 1: Did you give a clear picture of what happened in the first picture? (WH)

Check 2: Did you give a clear picture of what must have happened in the middle picture? (WH)

Check 3: Are all your sentences written correctly? (CP, DID, RO)

161

	Sam and Ann were on the bank of a wide
	river. Ann was picking up rocks. Sam was
	watching her. Ann threw one of the rocks.
CP	It almost went to the other side of the
WH	river. Sam picked up a rock and threw it as
	hard as he could. The rock did not go as
	far as the rock that Ann threw. Ann just
	smiled. When Sam saw that his rock did
COM	not go very far, Sam said, "My arm is sore."
	Ann threw another rock. This rock went
	even further than the first rock she threw.

Idea: Sam said, "I can throw rocks farther than you can."

Check 1: Do your sentences about picture 1 tell where Sam and Ann were and what they were doing? (WH)

Check 2: Do your sentences for the other pictures tell what Sam did and what Ann did? (WH, DID)

Check 3: Do you have at least two sentences for each picture? (WH)

162

	The mother fish grabbed the fishing line
RO	in her mouth. The mother fish got angry.
	~~and~~ S̲he swam away from the boat as fast
	as she could swim. Jim felt a tug on the
	fishing line. He held on to the fishing pole.
WH DID	Rhonda dropped the net and ~~grab~~ grabbed the oars.

Idea: The mother fish pulled Jim into the water.

Check 1: Did you write sentences that give a clear picture of what must have happened in the middle picture? (WH)

Check 2: Are all your sentences written correctly? (CP, DID, RO)

	Fred and the monkey were inside the
	monkey's cage. Fred was sitting on a tree
WH	stump. Fred yawned and said, "I think I'll
	take a nap." As Fred yawned, the monkey
	started to climb down the rope. In a few
CP	moments, Fred fell asleep. W̲hen the monkey
	saw that Fred was asleep, it pushed the
	cage door open and walked out of the cage.
COM	When Fred woke up, he looked around and
	said, "Where is that monkey?" The monkey
	sat on top of the cage and smiled.

Idea: The monkey was swinging on a rope.

Check 1: Do your sentences about picture 1 tell where Fred and the monkey were and what they were doing? (WH)

Check 2: Do your sentences for the other pictures tell what somebody or something did? (WH, DID)

Check 3: Do you have at least one sentence that begins with a part that tells when? (W, COM)

	The sheriff took a shower at the end
RO	of a hard day of work. ~~and a~~ A̲ deputy came
	in to the shower room. The deputy said,
Q	"We have an emergency call." The sheriff
	got ready as fast as he could. He hurried
WH	out of the shower and grabbed a towel. He
	picked up the emergency tool kit and ran
	outside in his bare feet. He ran towards
	the police car. His deputy put a leash on
	the dog. He also grabbed the sheriff's
	shoes and socks. The deputy and the dog
DID	~~run~~ ran after the sheriff.

Idea: He put on his uniform.

Check 1: Did you give a clear picture of what happened in the first picture? (WH)

Check 2: Did you correctly punctuate the sentence that tells what somebody said? (Q)

Check 3: Did you give a clear picture of what must have happened in the middle picture? (WH)

Check 4: Are all your sentences written correctly? (CP, RO, DID)

	Henry and Carlos decided to go
	fishing. They set their alarm clock before
	they went to sleep. The boys got up when
	the alarm clock went off. Carlos turned off
	the alarm clock.
	Henry and Carlos got out of bed and
	got dressed. They walked outside to their
	truck. They put the boat on the trailer.
	They drove the truck to the lake. When
COM	they arrived at the lake they took the
	boat off the trailer and put it in the water.
	Both boys put on their life jackets. Carlos
	carried the oars into the boat and climbed
	onto the front seat. Henry sat in the back
	seat with the fishing pole. Carlos rowed to
	the middle of the lake. He said, "We're
	going to be lucky today. I bet we catch ten
	fish."
W-1	A sentence that begins with a part that tells when

Check 1: Does your first paragraph give a clear picture of what happened in the first picture? (WH)

Check 2: Does your second paragraph give a clear picture of what happened in the middle picture and the last picture? (WH, P)

Check 3: Did you write at least two sentences that begin with a part that tells when? (W, COM)

	Roger took off his boots and went to
WH	sleep on a cot inside the tent. The baby
	monkey took the key from the table and
DID	walked over to the cage. It ~~open~~ opened the lock
	with the key. The mother monkey pushed
	the cage door open and walked out of the
	cage. The two monkeys walked to the
WH	table. The monkeys climbed up the tree
CP	to a branch that was over the tent. Roger
	slept the whole time.

Idea: The baby monkey climbed down the tree.

Idea: They grabbed some bananas from the table.

Check 1: Did you write sentences that give a clear picture of what must have happened in the middle picture? (WH)

Check 2: Are all your sentences written correctly? (CP, DID, RO)

167

168

	When the bridge broke, Tom fell into the
	stream. He stood up in the water. He said,
Q	"That water is cold. ✱ I am freezing." He
CP	climbed out of the stream. ^H he carried
	several logs to a campfire pit and built a
	fire. He took off his wet clothes and boots.
WH	He took a blanket from his tent and put it
DID	over him. He ~~walk~~ walked over to the fire to get
	warm.

Idea: He hung his wet clothes on a rope tied between two trees.

Check 1: Did you give a clear picture of what happened in the first picture? (WH)

Check 2: Did you correctly punctuate the sentence that tells what somebody said? (Q)

Check 3: Did you give a clear picture of what must have happened in the middle picture? (WH)

Check 4: Are all your sentences written correctly? (CP, RO, DID)

RO	Carla rode her bike over to the tree. ~~and~~
	^S she got off her bike. She leaned the bike
WH	against the tree. The monkey climbed up
	the tree and walked out onto a branch near
	the kite. The monkey shook the branches
DID	near the kite. The kite came loose. It ~~float~~ floated
	into the air. Carla decided to give a treat
CP	to the monkey. ^S she took out some bananas
	that were in the basket of her bike.

Idea: She took the chain off the monkey's neck.

Check 1: Did you write sentences that give a clear picture of what must have happened in the middle picture? (WH)

Check 2: Are all your sentences written correctly? (CP, DID, RO)

169

170

	Jerry's friends had a big lunch at Jerry's
CP	house. They left at 1 o'clock. The kitchen
	was a mess. Jerry's mom opened the
	kitchen door and said, "Please clean the
Q	kitchen while I go shopping." She went to
	the grocery store. Jerry worked hard while
RO	she was gone. ~~and~~ ^H he carried the dirty
	dishes from the table to the sink. He
WH	cleaned the table. He mopped the floor. He
	took out the garbage. He finished cleaning
	at 4 o'clock.

Idea: He washed the dishes and put them away.

Check 1: Did you give a clear picture of what happened in the first picture? **(WH)**

Check 2: Did you correctly punctuate the sentence that tells what somebody said? **(Q)**

Check 3: Did you give a clear picture of what must have happened in the middle picture? (WH)

Check 4: Are all your sentences written correctly? **(CP, RO, DID)**

42

RO	Alex ran onto the thin ice. ~~and~~ _the_ ice
WH	broke. He could not climb out of the water.
	Sally skated over to the barricade. She
	took the long board from the barricade.
CP	She put the board on the ice. _S_he held one
	end of the board. She slid the other end
DID	to the hole in the ice. Alex ~~climb~~ _climbed_ onto the
	board.
	Idea: Alex fell into the icy water.

Check 1: Did you write sentences that give a clear picture of what must have happened in the middle picture? (WH)

Check 2: Are all your sentences written correctly? (CP, DID, RO)

171

	Jill had almost finished painting the
RO	porch rail. ~~and~~ _Her_ mother came to the
Q	door. She said, "_G_et ready for your piano
DID	lesson." Jill ~~finish~~ _finished_ painting the rail and
	cleaned up her mess. She put the paint
	brushes in the paint cleaner. She put the
	lid on the paint. She also folded the rags.
	She took off her work boots and went
WH	inside. She sat on the piano bench with her
	mother.
	Idea: She changed into a pink dress and white shoes.

Check 1: Did you give a clear picture of what happened in the first picture? (WH)

Check 2: Did you correctly punctuate the sentence that tells what somebody said? (Q)

Check 3: Did you give a clear picture of what must have happened in the middle picture? (WH)

Check 4: Are all your sentences written correctly? (CP, RO, DID)

172

	The rock hit the hornet's nest.
WH	Hundreds of hornets came out of the
RO	nest. ~~and~~ _The_ angry hornets flew toward
CPWH	James. The hornets almost caught him.
	Idea: The nest fell to the ground.
	Idea: James ran toward the stream.

Check 1: Did you write sentences that give a clear picture of what must have happened in the middle picture? (WH)

Check 2: Are all your sentences written correctly? (CP, DID, RO)

173

	Ted was repairing a fence when he heard
	a car making funny noises. Mrs. Smith
	stood next to the car. Smoke was coming
Q	from the engine. Mrs. Smith said, "Can you
	help me? I'm having trouble with my car."
CP	Ted tried to help. _H_e lifted up the hood. He
	made the engine stop smoking but could
WH	not get the car to start. Mrs. Smith
	steered the car as Ted pulled the car with
	his tractor.
	Idea: He tied one end of a rope to the front of the car and the other end to the tractor.

Check 1: Did you give a clear picture of what happened in the first picture? (WH)

Check 2: Did you correctly punctuate the sentence that tells what somebody said? (Q)

Check 3: Did you give a clear picture of what must have happened in the middle picture? (WH)

Check 4: Are all your sentences written correctly? (CP, RO, DID)

174

Passage (top left)

	Tracy and Maria rode their snowmobile
	near a frozen lake. Nobody lived near this
RO	*lake. and the snowmobile hit a large rock*
	that was covered with snow. The
	snowmobile was damaged and couldn't run.
	Maria said, "We'll freeze unless we get
P	*out of the cold." The girls decided to build*
	an igloo. They took the tool kit from the
WH	*snowmobile. They stacked up the blocks of*
	ice to make an igloo. When they were
	finished, it was snowing. As Tracy started
Q	*to crawl inside the igloo, Maria said, "We'll*
	be a lot warmer when we get inside."
	Idea: The girls took the saw from the tool case and used the saw to cut the blocks of ice.

Check 1: Does your first paragraph give a clear picture of what happened before the first picture and in the first picture? (WH)

Check 2: Does your second paragraph give a clear picture of what happened in the middle picture and the last picture? (WH, P)

Check 3: Are all your sentences written correctly? (CP, RO, DID, Q)

Passage (top right)

	Jerry and his friends were in the
	kitchen. They were eating a big lunch. They
	finished lunch at 1 o'clock. The kitchen
	was a mess. As Jerry's friends were
COM	*leaving, Jerry's mom opened the kitchen*
	door. She said, "Please clean the kitchen
P	*while I go shopping." Jerry worked hard*
	while his mom went shopping for groceries.
	He carried the dirty dishes from the table
DID	*to the sink. He cleaned the table. He washed*
	all the dishes and put them away. He
	mopped the floor. He took out the garbage.
	He finished cleaning at 4 o'clock. His mom
	walked into the room just as he finished
	cleaning. Jerry said, "Everything is cleaned
	up. What's for dinner?"
W-1	A sentence that begins with a part that tells when

Additional Practice
Test 1

A Put in the capitals and periods.

A girl threw a ball to her brother. She threw the ball too hard. It rolled into the street. The boy started to run into the street. A truck moved toward the boy. A woman saw the truck. She grabbed the boy. The truck ran over the ball. The woman told the boy to be more careful.

B Fix up the passage so that each sentence begins with a capital and ends with a period.

A man took a big egg out of a nest. The man brought the egg to his house. He thought that the egg might be worth a lot of money. The doorbell rang. The man walked to the door. He opened the door. A big bird flew into the room. It picked up the egg. The man fainted. The big bird flew away with the egg.

C Fix up each sentence so that it tells what the persons did.

1. They ~~were wearing~~ wore helmets.
2. She ~~was throwing~~ threw the ball.
3. They ~~were cleaning~~ cleaned the room.
4. The boys ~~were sitting~~ sat on the floor.
5. He ~~was wearing~~ wore a new shirt.
6. The clown ~~was rubbing~~ rubbed his nose.

sat	threw	rubbed	wore	cleaned

D Fix up each sentence so that it tells what the person or thing did.

1. The boy ~~was chasing~~ chased a dog.
2. The girl ~~was washing~~ washed the car.
3. He ~~was writing~~ wrote a letter.
4. She ~~was eating~~ ate apples.
5. The airplane ~~was taking~~ took off.

took	chased	wrote	ate	washed

E Fill in the blank next to each sentence with *he, she, it* or *they.*

1. The man and the woman ate lunch.
2. Latrell and Kedrick walked on the sand.
3. The truck had a flat tire.
4. The apples cost 84 cents.
5. The woman wore a red shirt.
6. The old book was worth a lot of money.
7. Alberto and his dog went jogging.
8. The old man wore a long blue coat.

1. **They** ate lunch.
2. **They** walked on the sand.
3. **It** had a flat tire.
4. **They** cost 84 cents.
5. **She** wore a red shirt.
6. **It** was worth a lot of money.
7. **They** went jogging.
8. **He** wore a long blue coat.

F Fill in the blank next to each sentence with *he, she, it* or *they.*

1. A cat and a dog made a mess.
2. The girls went to school.
3. My mother was very pretty.
4. Rodney and his brother were not home.
5. Four ducks swam on the lake.
6. The tables were old.
7. My brother came home late.
8. That car was bright red.

1. **They** made a mess.
2. **They** went to school.
3. **She** was very pretty.
4. **They** were not home.
5. **They** swam on the lake.
6. **They** were old.
7. **He** came home late.
8. **It** was bright red.

G Circle the subject of each sentence. Underline the predicate.

1. (Five cats) were on the roof.
2. (They) read two funny books.
3. (A red bird) landed on a roof.
4. (A dog and a cat) played in their yard.
5. (It) stopped.

H Circle the subject of each sentence. Underline the predicate.

1. (Sara and Harry) painted the kitchen blue.
2. (Sara) had a paintbrush.
3. (Harry) used a roller.
4. (They) stopped to eat lunch.
5. (She) laughed.
6. (The windows) were blue.

Test 2

A Read the paragraph. Fix up any run-ons.

Nancy Wilson and Jane Robinson lived in a big city. ~~and~~ T they wanted to visit a friend who lived on a farm. The girls worked every day after school to earn money for the trip. ~~and~~ Nancy helped Mr. Jackson fix his car. Jane helped Mr. Baker paint his apartment. ~~and then~~ Nancy and Jane soon had enough money for the trip.

B Read the paragraph. Fix up any run-ons.

Yuri and Bill found a little bird that had fallen out of its nest. ~~and then~~ T they took the little bird home with them. Mr. Robinson gave them a book about birds. ~~and~~ T the book told how to take care of the bird. Yuri fed the bird while Bill made a bed for it. ~~and then~~ T the bird got better. Yuri and Bill took it back to its nest.

C Write the verb for each sentence.

1. She stopped the car.   **stopped**
2. A young man was walking on the path.   **was walking**
3. That truck had a flat tire.   **had**
4. Linda and Sandy were eating apples.   **were eating**
5. Everybody clapped.   **clapped**
6. He sat near the door.   **sat**

D Write the verb for each sentence.

1. She painted her room.   **painted**
2. They were sitting on the floor.   **were sitting**
3. His shirt was not dirty.   **was**
4. He was helping his mother.   **was helping**
5. A cow and a horse ate the grass.   **ate**
6. That nice woman helped us.   **helped**

E Rewrite each item with an apostrophe **s**.

1. The car belonged to **my uncle.** The car had a flat tire.
   My uncle's car had a flat tire.
2. The cat belonged to **her friend.** The cat was sleeping.
   Her friend's cat was sleeping.
3. The hat belonged to **Jill.** The hat was on the table.
   Jill's hat was on the table.
4. The toy belonged to **the baby.** The toy was broken.
   The baby's toy was broken.

F Rewrite each item with an apostrophe **s**.

1. The book belonged to **Jean.** The book had two hundred pages.
   Jean's book had two hundred pages.
2. The glasses belonged to **my sister.** The glasses were dirty.
   My sister's glasses were dirty.
3. The shirt belonged to **the teacher.** The shirt had red and white stripes.
   My teacher's shirt had red and white stripes.
4. The leg belonged to **Ray.** The leg was broken.
   Ray's leg was broken.

G Fill in the blanks with the correct words.

Three women worked on a house.

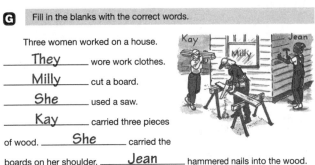

__They__ wore work clothes.

__Milly__ cut a board.

__She__ used a saw.

__Kay__ carried three pieces

of wood. __She__ carried the

boards on her shoulder. __Jean__ hammered nails into the wood.

H Fill in the blanks with the correct words.

__James__ and

__Alice__ were working.

__They__ were doing yard

work. __James__ sawed a

branch from a tree. __He__

wore a hat and work clothes.

__He__ held the branch with

one hand. __Alice__ dug a hole

in the dirt.

Test 3

A The number after each sentence tells how many mistakes. Fix up the mistakes.

1. ~~t~~he boys ~~good~~ went to Bills' house. (3)
2. Alice fell asleep.~~,~~ ̷she was very tired. (2)
3. ~~t~~hat boys' shirt has six red buttons and four yellow buttons. (3)
4. My best friends are ̷jerry ̷gomez and ̷alex ̷jordan. (4)
5. Melissa and ̷richard put their dog on ̷richard's bed. (3)
6. We looked outside.~~and~~ ~~T~~he rain had just stopped. (2)

B

1. My dad's cat had four kittens. (2)
2. She ~~taught~~ taught ̷robert and ̷jerry how to ride a bike. (3)
3. ̷she washed the windows of her dad's car. (3)
4. We ~~seen~~ saw ̷mrs. ̷jordan in the store. ̷she waved to us. (5)

C

__Ann__ and

__Kim__ were swimming.

__Ann__ wore a bathing cap.

__She__ also wore a watch.

__Jane__ sat near the water.

__She__ wore sunglasses.

__Sally__ stood next to the

blanket. __She__ wore shorts.

__She__ read a book.

D

__Jerry__ and __Al__ picked apples from

a tree. __Jerry__ wore a hat. __He__ had a

beard. __Al__ stood on a box. __He__ held a

bucket. __Sam__ and __Bill__ sat on a blanket.

__Sam__ read a book. __Bill__ wore a shirt with the

number 9 on the back. __He__ drew a picture.

E Circle the subject in each sentence.
Write **P** in front of each sentence that has a pronoun for a subject.

____ 1. (The tree) was beautiful.

_P_ 2. (He) ate pizza for dinner.

____ 3. (Those dogs) chased our cat.

____ 4. (Tina) read a book.

_P_ 5. (It) fell off the table.

_P_ 6. (They) bought new shirts.

____ 7. (My sister) painted the room.

____ 8. (Robert) finished his homework.

F Circle the subject in each sentence.
Write **P** in front of each sentence that has a pronoun for a subject.

____ 1. (Linda's shirt) was dirty.

_P_ 2. (They) painted the door.

_P_ 3. (He) is ten years old.

____ 4. (A new girl) walked into our class.

_P_ 5. (It) had big tires.

____ 6. (A boy and his friend) went to the store.

____ 7. (My little brother) is seven years old.

_P_ 8. (She) walked to school.

G Put in an apostrophe if the underlined object belongs to someone.

1. six <u>chairs</u>
2. my father's <u>chairs</u>
3. my father's <u>chair</u>
4. some <u>apples</u>
5. that tree's <u>leaves</u>
6. a car's <u>headlights</u>

7. a boy's <u>kites</u>
8. two big <u>oranges</u>
9. those red <u>cars</u>
10. that boy's <u>books</u>
11. the teachers' <u>pencil</u>
12. the tallest <u>girls</u>

H Put in an apostrophe if the underlined object belongs to someone.

1. a girl's <u>hairbrush</u>
2. that cat's <u>tail</u>
3. the birds in the <u>tree</u>
4. the bugs on the <u>table</u>
5. those cats near <u>John</u>

6. an old man's <u>face</u>
7. the woman's <u>umbrella</u>
8. many <u>cups</u>
9. a girl's <u>suitcase</u>

Test 4

A Write **N** above each noun.
Write **P** above each pronoun.
Write **V** above each verb.

1. They talked to her. (P V P)
2. A little cat sat next to him. (N V P)
3. The rain made them sad. (N V P)
4. He saw it. (P V P)

B Write **N** above each noun.
Write **P** above each pronoun.
Write **V** above each verb.

1. Linda helped him. (N V P)
2. They were next to her. (P V P)
3. My teacher saw it. (N V P)
4. That new book helped them. (N V P)

C The number after each item tells how many mistakes are in the item. Fix up the mistakes.

1. James said,"Today is my birthday. We are having a party." (2)
2. Bill met Alice in the park. She said,"You look good." (4)
3. Ann's dad is very tall. He plays basketball. (3)
4. The doctor said,"You have a bad cold. Don't go outside." (4)
5. I saw seen Ann and Jane at Mr. Jordan's house. (5)

D The number after each item tells how many mistakes are in the item. Fix up the mistakes.

1. Mr. Roberts said,"That is his bike." (3)
2. The boys went to Bill's house. (2)
3. That boy's shirt has six red buttons and four yellow buttons. (3)
4. My best friends are Jerry Gomez and Alex Jordan. (4)
5. Melissa and Richard put their dog on Richard's bed. (3)
6. He said," I am hungry. I want an apple." (4)

Test 5

A Write **N** above each underlined noun.
Write **P** above each underlined pronoun.
Write **V** above each underlined verb.

1. He bought a new shirt at the store. (P V N N)
2. Yesterday morning, we saw her. (N P V P)
3. My school had a big playground. (N V N)
4. A girl painted her room. (N V N)

B Write **N** above each underlined noun.
Write **P** above each underlined pronoun.
Write **V** above each underlined verb.

1. She stood in front of the table. (P V N)
2. In the morning, she ate an apple. (N P V N)
3. The water dripped on it. (N V P)
4. After the party, she walked to her house. (N P V N)

C For each sentence, circle the subject and underline the whole predicate.

1. Before the sun went down, (the birds) began to sing.
2. (Jason and Robert) fell asleep after a few minutes.
3. After school, (we) walked home.
4. Last night, (everybody) went to sleep early.
5. (We) had eggs for breakfast.

D For each sentence, circle the subject and underline the whole predicate.

1. When the light turned green, (she) put her foot on the gas pedal.
2. After dinner, (my dad) took a nap.
3. (He) felt very tired when he got home.
4. Before school, (we) played on the bars.
5. (My brother and my sister) were at school.

E For each sentence, fill in the blank with the word **asked** or the word **said.** Then make the correct ending mark.

1. Her friend ___said___ , "That was a good meal. "
2. Jane ___asked___ , "Did it rain?"
3. He ___asked___ , "Are you hungry?"
4. Jason ___said___ , "Nobody is home. "

F For each sentence, fill in the blank with the word **asked** or the word **said.** Then make the correct ending mark.

1. He ___asked___ , "Is lunch ready?"
2. They ___asked___ , "Did you see her?"
3. Alice ___asked___ , "Where is Adams Avenue?"
4. He ___said___ , "It's time to eat. "

G Put a comma in each sentence that begins with the part that tells when.

1. The boys went home after school.
2. During the rainstorm, our dog hid under the bed.
3. After we fixed the car, we made dinner.
4. In the morning, Jane walked to school.
5. That girl was happy when she got her report card.
6. He fell asleep while he read a book.
7. After James sat down, the music started.

H Put a comma in each sentence that begins with the part that tells when.

1. A cat jumped up when the alarm clock rang.
2. When we got home, the dog started barking.
3. In the morning, we ate breakfast.
4. While the baby slept, we talked quietly.
5. Her brother was happy when he got the letter.
6. They finished the job just before midnight.
7. Before they made lunch, the cooks washed their hands.

Test 7

A Write **V** above each verb.
Write **N** above each noun.
Write **A** above each adjective.

1. Four cats slept on the big pillow.
2. An old man drove a new car.
3. That smart girl knew every answer.

B Write **V** above each verb.
Write **N** above each noun.
Write **A** above each adjective.

1. A young boy jumped into the deep water.
2. Her uncle had a friendly dog.
3. Tom helped his little sister.

C Fix up each sentence so it is punctuated correctly.

1. The flag was red, white and blue. (1)
2. My brother, my mother and my sister had colds. (1)
3. James opened the door, put on his coat and walked down the stairs. (1)

D Fix up each sentence so it is punctuated correctly.

1. We found two bottles, three cans and six coins. (1)
2. Raymond, his sister and Carmen went skating. (1)
3. Jean turned off the radio, closed the window and turned on the heater. (1)

E Capitalize all parts of any item that names one person or one place.

1. a big city
2. Burnside Avenue
3. Bumpo Car Company
4. that lake
5. Mississippi River
6. Dr. Mitchell
7. an old house
8. Los Angeles

F Capitalize all parts of any item that names one person or one place.

1. my sister
2. Oak Street
3. New York
4. United States
5. this country
6. his street
7. Dr. Evans
8. Delto Stove Company

G Fill in each blank with the verb **was** or **were.**

1. Sandy and her mother ___were___ on the bus.
2. She ___was___ on the bus.
3. The girl's arm ___was___ sore.
4. You ___were___ wise to buy that book.
5. Three men ___were___ in the boat.

H Fill in each blank with the verb **was** or **were**.

1. Ellen's son ___was___ sick.
2. You ___were___ wrong.
3. They ___were___ at school.
4. James and I ___were___ in the house.
5. The boy's teacher ___was___ happy.
6. You ___were___ first in line.

Test 8

A Write **V** above each verb. Write **N** above each noun. Write **P** above each pronoun. Write **A** above each adjective.

1. When the bell rang, we went to our classroom.
   (A N — P V — A N)
2. Linda stood in front of a large desk.
   (N V — A A N)
3. That tiny black fly flew into my cup.
   (A A A N V — A N)
4. During the night, a strong wind blew.
   (A N — A A N V)

B

1. During the big storm, we went inside an old house.
   (A A N — P V — A A N)
2. He saw many black ants on the kitchen table.
   (P V A A N — A N)
3. Two old men helped her.
   (A A N V P)
4. His truck moved slowly up a steep hill.
   (P N V — A A N)
5. After the meeting, she went to the store.
   (A N — P V — A N)

C The number after each sentence tells how many mistakes. Fix up the mistakes.

1. The mississippi river is the longest river in the united states. (4)
   (M R U S)
2. Texas, alaska and california are the biggest states. (3)
   (A C)
3. Is los angeles bigger than san francisco? (4)
   (L A S F)
4. We lived on baldwin street until last september. (3)
   (B S S)
5. After she brushed her teeth, she went to bed. (2)
   (S)
6. My favorite cities are new york, dallas and miami. (5)
   (N Y D M)
7. Ann asked mr. james, "Where can I buy that book?" (7)
   (M J I ?")

D

1. The empire state building is in new york. (5)
   (E S B N Y)
2. Robert fed the dog, washed the dishes and cleaned his room before lunch. (1)
3. Is mexico larger than canada? (3)
   (M C ?)
4. Jill asked, "Where is Dr. Lee's office?" (2)
5. I bought apples, oranges and pears at the store. (1)
6. December, january and february are the coldest months of the year. (3)
   (J F)
7. Yoko's sister lives on washington street. (3)
   (W S)
8. Tom and his sister ~~was~~ were in the park. (1)

Test 9

A

1. Write the date for the fifth day of August in the year 1968.
   ___August 5, 1968___
2. Write the date for the third day of June in the year 2001.
   ___June 3, 2001___
3. Write the date for the eleventh day of March in the year 1792.
   ___March 11, 1792___
4. Write the date for the eighth day of July in the year 1812.
   ___July 8, 1812___
5. Write the date for the nineteenth day of November in the year 1947.
   ___November 19, 1947___

B

1. Write the date for the 21st day of May in the year 1886.
   ___May 21, 1886___
2. Write the date for the seventeenth day of September in the year 2010.
   ___September 17, 2010___
3. Write the date for the tenth day of January in the year 1935.
   ___January 10, 1935___
4. Write the date for the 23rd day of March in the year 1722.
   ___March 23, 1722___

C

1. Greenville Iowa ___Greenville, Iowa___

2. Street number: 45
   Street name: Vine Street
   City name: Greenville
   State name: Iowa
   Write the address with commas.
   ___45 Vine Street, Greenville, Iowa___

3. Street number: 7
   Street name: Old Goat Road
   City name: Chico
   State name: California
   Write the address with commas.
   ___7 Old Goat Road, Chico, California___

Test 11

A Write **sing** or **sings** in each blank. Write **one** or **more than one** after each sentence.

1. His dad _____sings_____ well. _____one_____

2. His dad and mom _____sing_____ well. more than one

3. Those ten kids _____sing_____ well. more than one

4. Her older brothers _____sing_____ well. more than one

B Write **like** or **likes** in each blank. Write **one** or **more than one** after each sentence.

1. My friend's dad _____likes_____ spinach. _____one_____

2. The women _____like_____ to fish. more than one

3. They _____like_____ our cat. more than one

4. She _____likes_____ to run. _____one_____

Textbook Answer Key

Lesson 17
Part C

1. (Idea:) The candle landed on the newspapers. The newspapers start to burn. The woman picked up a bucket of water.

Part D

1. Rode.
2. Was singing.
3. Slipped.
4. Was eating.
5. Sat.
6. Played.

Lesson 18
Part C

1. (Idea:) The horse jumped over the corral fence. Bill fell off the horse. Lisa jumped down from the fence and grabbed the rope.

Part D

1. Was playing.
2. Stopped.
3. Were talking.
4. Ate.
5. Were sleeping.
6. Felt.

Lesson 19
Part A

1. (Idea:) The baker swung his flyswatter at the fly. The flyswatter hit the pie. The pie splattered all over the baker. The fly flew away.

Part B

1. Fell.
2. Whispered.
3. Were eating.
4. Was sitting.
5. Stopped.
6. Were sleeping.

Part C

1. Two butterflies landed on a cow's head.
2. The paint dripped onto Sam's shirt.
3. A mouse sat on Milly's shoe.
4. A boy sat on his father's knee.

Lesson 21
Part C

1. The ball went between Tom's legs.
2. Two birds stood on a woman's arm.
3. The monkey pulled a lion's tail.
4. A girl combed her mother's hair.

Lesson 23
Part C

1. Sat.
2. Were talking.
3. Walked.
4. Was making.
5. Were.
6. Had.

Part D

1. Stan said, "My foot feels better."
2. Miss Woods said, "I am hungry."
3. A boy said, "It is very late."

Lesson 24
Part C

1. Drank, sat, played, gave, kicked.

Part D

1. Ann said, "I like to play in the grass."
2. Kenny said, "This popcorn is salty."
3. A clown said, "I can make you laugh."

Lesson 25
Part D

1. Mr. Webster said, "We are almost there."
2. Liz said, "My kite is stuck in that tree."
3. The boy said, "I like to read."

Lesson 26
Part D

1. Mr. Simms said, "My car is dirty."
2. The woman said, "I need a new book."
3. Heather said, "This water is cold."

Lesson 27
Part C

1. Fell.
2. Is sitting.
3. Went.
4. Stopped.
5. Were moving.
6. Has.

Part D

1. The mechanic said, "This car is almost fixed."
2. Miss Winston said, "You need some help."
3. Randy said, "It has been raining all day."

Lesson 28
Part C

1. Pronoun.
2. Verb.
3. Pronoun.
4. Pronoun.
5. Verb.
6. Verb.
7. Pronoun.

Part D

1. The girl said, "It is time to eat."
2. Mary said, "Your dog has a sore leg."
3. My brother said, "You look sick."

Lesson 29
Part C

1. Pronoun.
2. Verb.
3. Pronoun.
4. Verb.
5. Pronoun.
6. Verb.
7. Pronoun.
8. Pronoun.

Part D

1. His mother said, "What do you want?"
2. He said, "Are you feeling better?"
3. Jim said, "These shoes are too big."
4. She said, "Where is the car?"

Lesson 33
Part C

1. Verb.
2. Pronoun.
3. Pronoun.
4. Verb.
5. Pronoun.
6. Pronoun.
7. Verb.
8. Pronoun.

Part D

1. Dog.
2. Girls.
3. Friend.
4. Movie.
5. James.

Lesson 34
Part D

1. Verb.
2. Pronoun.
3. Pronoun.
4. Verb.
5. Pronoun.
6. Verb.

Part E

1. Shirt.
2. Cats.
3. Dream.
4. Mary.
5. Table.

Lesson 35
Part C

1. In the morning, they went swimming.
2. While the baby slept, we talked softly.
3. After lunch, the cook took a nap.

Part D

1. His mother said, "We need some milk. Will you go to the store?"
2. Doug said, "Can I go outside? It is snowing."
3. Abby said, "We went to the zoo. The monkeys made us laugh."

Lesson 36
Part C

1. James said, "I live in Texas. Where do you live?"
2. Sally said, "My brother will meet us. He will bring the boat."

Part D

1. While Jane went shopping, they cleaned the kitchen.
2. In the morning, he read a book.
3. After the rain stopped, the sun came out.
4. As she walked into the room, she tripped.

Lesson 37
Part C

1. Pronoun.
2. Verb.
3. Pronoun.
4. Pronoun.
5. Verb.
6. Pronoun.
7. Pronoun.
8. Verb.

Part D

1. As she walked to school, she sang a song.
2. When the bell rang, Jerry woke up.
3. During the night, a big wind blew.
4. All winter long, the bears slept.
5. Before suppertime, she was tired.

Lesson 38
Part D

1. When the sun came up, birds sang.
2. As Tim walked into the room, everybody laughed.
3. After he brushed his teeth, he went to sleep.
4. After fixing the fence, they ate lunch.

Lesson 39
Part D

2. After Tina fed the dog, she walked down the stairs.
3. After Tina walked down the stairs, she talked to the mail carrier.
4. After Tina talked to the mail carrier, she got into her car.

Lesson 42
Part D

1. At one o'clock, Bill ate lunch.
2. At four o'clock, Bill went outside.

Lesson 45
Part C

2. After James brushed his teeth, he combed his hair.
3. After James combed his hair, he washed his face.

Lesson 46
Part C

1. Now or At last.
2. Next.
3. Suddenly.
4. Now or At last.

Lesson 49
Part C

1. A, C or D.
2. A.
3. A or C.

Lesson 50
Part A

(Two sentences should begin with a part that tells when. Each sentence should have a comma after the part that tells when.)

Part B

1. A or B.
2. C or D.
3. C.

Lesson 51
Part D

1. (Idea:) The house had broken windows. The house had a chimney.

Lesson 52
Part C

1. The boy ran, slipped on the ice and fell down.
2. John, Mary and Jim went jogging.
3. They were tired, thirsty and hungry.

Part D

1. (Idea:) The hat had a feather. The hat was large.

Lesson 53
Part C

1. My mother, my father and my brother were sleeping.
2. We ate cereal, eggs and pancakes for breakfast.
3. I bought an apple, an orange and a peach.

Part D

1. (Idea:) Three girls were in front of a large house. They were sitting on the grass. They were reading books.
2. (Idea:) Two girls were in front of a small house. They were jumping rope.

Lesson 54
Part B

1. Two women were inside a house. They were standing on the stairs and painting a wall.
2. Three women were outside a house. They were sitting on the front steps and petting a dog.

Lesson 55
Part B

1. Name.
2. Day.
3. Month.
4. Month.
5. Day.
6. Name.

Part C

1. (Idea:) The man painted a table, a chair and a door.
2. (Idea:) The woman wore sandals, a bathing suit and a hat.
3. (Idea:) The man carried a saw, a hammer and a bag of nails.

Lesson 57
Part C

1. (Idea:) Rosa hung up the phone, put on her coat and went outside.
2. (Idea:) Jason picked up a dog, put the dog in the tub and turned on the water.

Lesson 58
Part C

1. (Idea:) A janitor washed the chalkboard, put a chair on the desk and swept the floor.

Lesson 59
Part C

1. (Idea:) Ann and Sue rode bicycles, jumped rope and climbed a tree.

Lesson 62
Part C

1. Our teacher.   _(A = Our, N = teacher)_
2. A man.   _(A = A, N = man)_
3. Nine red bugs.   _(A = Nine, A = red, N = bugs)_
4. My younger sister.   _(A = My, A = younger, N = sister)_

Part D

1. R.
2. No.
3. No.
4. R.
5. No.

Lesson 63
Part B

1. Seven little bugs.   _(A = Seven, A = little, N = bugs)_
2. Her best friend.   _(A = Her, A = best, N = friend)_
3. Dogs.   _(N = Dogs)_
4. An airplane.   _(A = An, N = airplane)_
5. Their mother.   _(A = Their, N = mother)_
6. His blue pants.   _(A = His, A = blue, N = pants)_

Part C

B, D.

Lesson 64
Part C

B, C, F.

Lesson 72
Part C

1. If they lose the game, they will be sad.
2. Unless he is sick, he will go with us.
3. Although she had a bad cold, she won the race.

Lesson 73
Part C

1. If we win the game, we will be very happy.
2. Unless she falls down, she will win the race.
3. Although it rained all night, the field was dry.

Lesson 74
Part D

1. Although she was not feeling well, she went to the show.
2. Unless it rains, we will go swimming.
3. If he keeps on eating so much, he will get sick.

Lesson 75
Part C

1. The dog started howling when we got home.
2. In the morning, the air was cold.
3. He took a nap after he ate lunch.
4. As he talked on the phone, he painted a picture.

Lesson 77
Part C

1. The lights came on when the car started.
2. On Monday night, we watched football.
3. She made dinner after she fixed the car.
4. While he was watching TV, he fell asleep.
5. Before she went to sleep, she brushed her teeth.

Lesson 78
Part C

1. We went to the park in the morning.
2. After the rain stopped, he ran home.
3. As she walked out the door, she put on a hat.
4. We stayed home on Saturday.
5. They milked the cows when they came home from school.

Lesson 79
Part C

1. By the end of the day, everybody was happy.
2. Before we went outside, we finished our work.
3. They talked about the movie as they walked home.
4. He felt sick when he woke up.

Lesson 84
Part A

1. 95
2. Supplies for the Race
3. 109
4. Al Learns About Molecules

Part B

1. Orlando, Florida
2. 485 Lake Avenue, Detroit, Michigan
3. 22 Hidden Valley Road, Cleveland, Ohio

Part C

1. answer
2. baby
3. don't
4. happen
5. monkey
6. only

Part D

1. disagree
2. disappear
3. dislike
4. dishonest

Lesson 88
Part B

1. captain
2. decide
3. enormous
4. forever
5. label
6. middle

Part C

1. disappear
2. restart
3. unclean
4. unfair
5. dislike
6. unaware

Lesson 89
Part B

1. 98
2. Rest Periods
3. 134
4. A Book About the Poles

Part C

1. effortless
2. homeless
3. disconnected
4. reconnect
5. unzipped
6. hatless

Lesson 90—Test 9
Part A

1. August 10, 1886

Part B

305 Market Street, Salem, Oregon

Part C

1. 93
2. A Practice Run

Part D

1. disapprove
2. unhappy
3. rewrite

Lesson 91
Part A

1. 136
2. Angela and Al Go to the Library
3. 82
4. On the Tour

Part B

1. treeless
2. formless
3. reapprove
4. disapprove
5. jointless
6. cloudless

Part C

1. ocean
2. officer
3. once
4. outfit
5. oven

Lesson 93
Part A

1. 329
2. 100
3. 266
4. 77
5. 163

Part B

1. beyond
2. billows
3. blew
4. boast
5. breath
6. building

Part C

1. harmful
2. displeased
3. voiceless
4. relight
5. joyless
6. joyful

Lesson 94
Part C

1. easy
2. edge
3. eggs
4. enormous
5. eraser
6. escape
7. evening
8. eyes

Part D

1. hardness
2. tenderness
3. disbelief
4. thoughtful
5. thoughtless
6. brightness
7. unhappy
8. pointless

Lesson 95
Part C

1. rewrite
2. fairness
3. disagree
4. unfinished
5. hopeless
6. freshness
7. closeness
8. coatless

Lesson 96
Part D

1. rider
2. sadness
3. thoughtful
4. disapprove
5. runner
6. joyless
7. dullness
8. undone
9. sleeveless
10. rebuild

Lesson 97
Part C

1. retype
2. meanness
3. rewash
4. washer
5. baker
6. tasteless
7. skillful
8. roundness
9. careless
10. taster

Lesson 98
Part B

1. hardness
2. superhard
3. coldness
4. supercold
5. discolored
6. recolor
7. tearful
8. tearless
9. brightness
10. superbright
11. unhealthy

Part C

1. Index
2. 330
3. It
4. 341
5. hurt

Lesson 99
Part B

1. sitter
2. narrowness
3. painless
4. firmness
5. superfirm
6. unfirm
7. giver
8. regive
9. waterless
10. speaker

Part C

1. Index
2. 163
3. old
4. 336
5. computer

Lesson 103
Part C

1. player
2. replay
3. playable
4. washable
5. washer
6. unwashed
7. lightness
8. disagree
9. manageable

Lesson 104
Part A

1. containers (Accept reasonable responses listing four kinds of containers A-D.)
2. games (Accept reasonable responses listing four kinds of games A-D.)
3. holidays (Accept reasonable responses listing four holidays A-D.)

Part B

1. amaze
2. banana
3. decide
4. early
5. electric
6. hundred
7. people
8. plastic
9. purple
10. special

Part C

1. readable
2. unread
3. hairless
4. painful
5. dishonest
6. believable
7. touchable
8. rewatch

Lesson 105
Part C

1. washable
2. miscount
3. starless
4. unseen
5. relabel
6. mislabel
7. walkable
8. toughness
9. misname

Lesson 106
Part A

1. coat
2. cob
3. cod
4. collar
5. complete
6. cone
7. cook
8. count

Part B

1. gentleness
2. misunderstand
3. joyful
4. misread
5. moveable
6. fearless
7. painter
8. uncooked
9. misplace

Lesson 107
Part A

1. draft
2. dream
3. driver
4. drop
5. drum
6. dry

Part B

1. mislead
2. strangeness
3. strangely
4. quietly
5. unfinished
6. disapprove
7. careful
8. sweetly
9. sunless

Lesson 108
Part A

1. certain
2. chip
3. circus
4. city
5. clipper

Part B

1. roughly
2. roughness
3. reclean
4. cleaner
5. hopeless
6. completely
7. misdo
8. kindly
9. readable

Lesson 109
Part A

1. chill
2. chin
3. chirp
4. chunk
5. circle
6. class
7. claw

Part B

1. redo
2. quietness
3. superbrave
4. unreal
5. worthless
6. follower
7. untold
8. calmness

Lesson 110—Test 11
Part A

1. raccoon
2. really
3. rose
4. track
5. turtle
6. twice

Part B

1. brightness
2. driver
3. treeless
4. superbright
5. sadly
6. washable
7. careful
8. misspell

Part C

1. like
2. drives
3. sing
4. writes
5. need

Lesson 111
Part B

1. husky, nerve
2. nightmare, scent

Part C

1. wingless
2. skater
3. unwritten
4. roadless
5. recut
6. unplanned
7. rudeness
8. listener

Lesson 112
Part A

1. cat   camp, cell
2. chest   cheap, chop
3. chart   chap, chat
4. care   camp, cell

Part B

1. uncut
2. smokeless
3. leader
4. disallow
5. unlit
6. slowness

Lesson 114
Part C

1. fact
2. opinion
3. opinion
4. opinion
5. fact
6. opinion
7. opinion
8. opinion

Lesson 115
Part A

1. go down
2. a tool
3. more than someone needs

Part B

1. opinion
2. fact
3. opinion
4. opinion
5. fact
6. opinion

Lesson 116
Part B

1. breakfast (Accept reasonable responses listing four kinds of breakfast A-D)
2. lunch (Accept reasonable responses listing four kinds of lunch A-D)
3. dinner (Accept reasonable responses listing four kinds of dinner A-D)

Part C

1. colorful bird
2. leftover food
3. clothing

Lesson 117
Part A

1. winter (Accept reasonable responses listing winter detail A-C)
2. spring (Accept reasonable responses listing spring detail A-C)
3. summer (Accept reasonable responses listing summer detail A-C)
4. fall (Accept reasonable responses listing fall detail A-C)

Part B

1. approved of
2. speed
3. small

Lesson 118
Part A

(Accept reasonable responses for three different ages with three to four activities specified for each age.)

Part B

1. take away
2. grains

Part C

1. dragonflies, horizon
2. cell, disk
3. nightmare, scent

Lesson 119
Part A

1. house
2. musical instrument

Part B

1. science, twilight
2. husky, nerve
3. absolutely, buoyant

Lesson 120
Part A

1. table of contents
2. index
3. glossary
4. table of contents
5. table of contents
6. index
7. table of contents

Part B

1. Partly burned coal
2. money spent

Lesson 121
Part A

1. return
2. teacher
3. superclean
4. brightness
5. disappear

Part B

1. index
2. index
3. table of contents
4. glossary
5. table of contents
6. index

Lesson 122
Part A

1. helpful
2. result
3. retain
4. contain
5. dismiss
6. unhappiness

Part B

1. table of contents
2. index
3. index
4. glossary
5. table of contents

Part C

1. a fish
2. pilot

Lesson 123
Part A

1. subjective
2. inject
3. detainment
4. reject
5. revert
6. inverted

Part B

1. index
2. glossary
3. table of contents
4. table of contents
5. index

Part C

1. cell, disk
2. unbearable, yucky
3. science, twilight

Lesson 124
Part A

1. produce
2. reply
3. reduce
4. diverting

Part B

1. index
2. glossary
3. index
4. glossary

Part C

1. Her teeth and pearls.
2. (Ideas:) Both were shiny; both were sparkling white.
3. Her eyes and diamonds.
4. (Ideas:) Both are shiny; both sparkle.
5. They and ants.
6. (Idea:) Both work hard.

Lesson 125
Part A

1. Similes
2. That man and a turtle.
3. (Idea:) Both moved slowly.
4. The team and a well-designed machine.
5. (Ideas:) Both work smoothly; they don't make mistakes.
6. They and deer.
7. (Idea:) Both are fast.
8. Her smile and the sun.
9. (Idea:) Both are warm.

Part B

1. mistake
2. smoothly
3. waterless
4. unhappiness
5. revisit
6. kissable

Part C

1. shallow water
2. a tree

Lesson 126
Part A

1. Her eyes and diamonds.
2. (Idea:) Both sparkle; both are shiny.
3. Her teeth and pearls.
4. (Ideas:) Both are white; both are shiny.
5. Her muscles and rocks.
6. (Idea:) Both are hard.

Part B

1. happy
2. poor
3. not clear

Part C

1. dishonestly
2. useful
3. misuse
4. refillable
5. recline
6. helpless
7. distress

Lesson 127
Part A

1. simile
2. metaphor
3. metaphor
4. simile
5. simile

Part B

1. not shy
2. not thoughtful
3. soft

Part C

1. entrance
2. plan

Lesson 128
Part A

1. metaphor
2. simile
3. metaphor
4. simile
5. simile
6. simile
7. metaphor

Part B

1. money
2. careful
3. very short
4. poor

Part C

1. (Idea:) A crop is a plant that is grown and harvested.
2. (Idea:) When you crop somebody's hair, you cut the outer parts.
3. (Idea:) When you stoop, you bend forward and down.
4. (Idea:) A stoop is a small porch.

Lesson 129
Part A

1. women
2. 3
3. (Idea:) To show or point
4. verb

Part B

1. (Idea:) A loom is a machine used to make cloth.
2. (Idea:) When something looms, it comes into view.
3. (Idea:) When you plant something, you put it in the ground to grow.
4. (Idea:) A plant is a factory.
5. (Idea:) A plain is a large, flat area of land with few trees.
6. (Idea:) Something is plain if it is not fancy.

Lesson 131
Part A

1. (Accept three words that start with the j sound.)
2. (Accept three words that start with the f sound.)
3. (Accept three words that start with the r sound.)
4. (Accept three words that start with the m sound.)

Part B

1. Egypt, pyramids
2. Socrates
3. Brazil
4. Benjamin Franklin

Part C

1. (Idea:) A pine is an evergreen tree.
2. (Idea:) When you pine, you suffer from longing.
3. (Idea:) A story is a report about an event.
4. (Idea:) A story is a floor in a building.

Lesson 132
Part A

1. New Orleans
2. reindeer
3. Alexander Graham Bell
4. Civil war

Part B

1. (Accept three words that start with the l sound.)
2. (Accept three words that start with the n sound.)
3. (Accept three words that start with the p sound.)
4. (Accept three words that start with the b sound.)

Part C

1. The lake and glass.
2. (Ideas:) Both were smooth and shiny; both were sparkling.
3. Her eyes and saucers.
4. (Idea:) Both are big and round.
5. Uncle Charlie and a bear.
6. (Ideas:) Both rock when they walk; both are not graceful; both take heavy steps.
7. The palm of his hand and sandpaper.
8. (Ideas:) Both are rough; both are scratchy.

Lesson 133
Part A

1. Great Lakes
2. France
3. Alaska
4. Illinois
5. Greece

Part C

1. table of contents
2. index
3. table of contents
4. index
5. glossary

Lesson 134
Part B

1. atlas
2. encyclopedia
3. dictionary
4. atlas
5. encyclopedia

Lesson 135
Part B

1. dictionary
2. encyclopedia
3. encyclopedia
4. dictionary
5. atlas

Part C

1. index
2. glossary
3. index
4. glossary